Artificial Intelligence for Managers

Leverage the Power of AI to Transform Organizations and Reshape Your Career

Malay A. Upadhyay

www.bpbonline.com

FIRST EDITION 2021

Copyright © BPB Publications, India

ISBN: 978-93-89898-385

LIMITS OF LIABILITY AND DISCLAIMER OF WARRANTY

Distributors:

BPB PUBLICATIONS
20, Ansari Road, Darya Ganj
New Delhi-110002
Ph: 23254990/23254991

DECCAN AGENCIES
4-3-329, Bank Street,
Hyderabad-500195
Ph: 24756967/24756400

MICRO MEDIA
Shop No. 5, Mahendra Chambers,
150 DN Rd. Next to Capital Cinema,
V.T. (C.S.T.) Station, MUMBAI-400 001
Ph: 22078296/22078297

BPB BOOK CENTRE
376 Old Lajpat Rai Market,
Delhi-110006
Ph: 23861747

To View Complete
BPB Publications Catalogue
Scan the QR Code:

Published by Manish Jain for BPB Publications, 20 Ansari Road, Darya Ganj, New Delhi-110002 and Printed by him at Repro India Ltd, Mumbai

www.bpbonline.com

Dedicated to

Those who would prefer to prepare for the future, than wait for it to happen

About the Author

Malay A. Upadhyay is a Customer Journey executive, certified in Machine Learning. Over the course of his role heading the function at a N. American AI SaaS firm in Toronto, Malay trained 150+ N. American managers on the basics of AI and its successful adoption, held executive thought leadership sessions for CEOs and CHROs on AI strategy & IT modernization roadmaps, and worked as the primary liaison to realize AI value on unique customer datasets. It was here that he learnt the growing need for greater knowledge and awareness of how to use AI both responsibly and successfully.

Malay was also one of 25 individuals chosen globally to envision the industrial future for the Marzotto Group, Italy, on its 175th anniversary. He holds an MBA, M.Sc. and B.E., with experiences across India, UAE, Italy and Canada.

A Duke of Edinburgh awardee, Malay has been driving the subject of responsible AI management as an advisor, author, online instructor and member of the European AI Alliance that informed the HLEG on the European Commission's AI policy. At other times, he remains a Fly that loves to travel and blog with Mrs. Fly.

About the Reviewer

 **Henry Bol** AI expert with domain knowledge in E-commerce and Online Marketing.

I feel very fortunate to have been active in Internet Business since the early days (1997): pioneering, learning by doing. In 2007, I started as an independent ecommerce expert: both as an ad interim professional to improve online marketing & sales or as a project manager for supervising internet projects. I am grateful of having had the opportunity to work at quite a few different and renowned companies.

Another important step is in 2017 (these seem to be every 10 years): seeing the big impact and magic of Artificial Intelligence, I started intensively studying AI. I covered the full range: from modelling to business models, from coding to ethics.

AI is bringing new dimensions to business and technology. Bridging those worlds is the challenge.

Contact details:
- henry@weareflow.com
- https://www.linkedin.com/in/henrybol/

What Some Students Have To Say

"I took up this course just because of my personal interest but now I feel that it has helped me explore new options and opportunities. I feel that it is a really good, helpful and interesting course for people who are curious to increase their knowledge of AI."

"This is a very useful AI course. Unlike several AI courses out there that are tech-heavy or more about coding, this course helps managers and leaders understand AI in an easier way. By the end of this course, I felt more confident about my knowledge of AI, how to understand or use it and how to successfully implement it in my company."

"Very informative and example based learning. The quizzes and examples help you retain useful information."

"An awesome course explaining complex concepts of AI in simple terms. Really helpful for any management students who want to get a good understanding of AI in the business world."

Acknowledgement

First and foremost, I would like to thank my parents, who had allowed a younger me to temporarily put aside my career as a trained engineer and marketer to pursue one as an author. This book, like others that came before it, is a result of that authorial first step that few parents would risk. I can't thank you enough.

A 'Thank You' must also go out to my wife, Pooja, for supporting every project I undertake, especially since they invariably demand the time that would otherwise be reserved for her.

I would also like to thank the team at BPB Publications, my publisher, for driving this book with inspiring process detail and receptivity, from an obscure Word document to your hands. And Henry Bol, whose feedback has lent this cake, its icing. It's been a pleasure.

Developing a thorough understanding in a field as little understood as AI requires a climate that can nurture knowledge-sharing and experience-gaining. For that, credit goes to my colleagues, our clients, and my instructors who have revealed the different facets and sensitivities of AI journeys along the way.

And of course, no task is ever accomplished without His/Her grace, whether we consider it bestowed upon us by an omnipresent entity or an elevated fragment of ourselves.

Thank you, Sai Baba.

Preface

Welcome to this journey on how to use and manage Artificial Intelligence.

Let's start with a story. Back in the 90s, I remember the day my family brought our first personal computer home. Everyone in the family looked at it with amazement. There weren't many users back then. People had only heard about it and were casually intrigued by it. But none of us knew that in a few years, each one of us would start using these computers and that it would become a core skill to know to avoid being left behind. Today this skill comes to us naturally.

Why am I sharing this with you? Because unlike computers back then, AI today is already a part of our everyday life, whether we realize it or not. It has become advanced enough to allow the creation of an entirely new organism (from frog stem cells) called Xenobots – tiny living machines that can move independently and even self-heal! And yet, organizations are struggling to find managers who can understand and get results out of even simple AI solutions at work. What does that tell us about the prevalent skill gap in AI management? And how important a role can AI plays in your life and career over the years?

There is a good reason for this growing importance of AI. As you will see through this course, artificial intelligence is solving problems that we just cannot solve without it: Problems that arise because of our reduced ability to focus, our need to analyze a lot of information quickly and cheaply, the rising costs and even a lack of time in our busy lives. Whether we think AI is dangerous or a gift, we have to understand it properly first. And that brings us to the problem at hand.

While we are trying to train more data scientists and engineers to create good AI solutions, there is a growing lack of users, managers, and leaders who know how to apply AI in their work or to business/organizational problems in the right manner. Most AI initiatives fail today not because of lack of good solutions but because of one or more of the following issues on the management side:

- Lack of understanding of what AI is and why/when it can be powerful
- Unrealistic expectations of what AI can do
- Absence of a proper business strategy in place around AI
- Wrong choice of the type of AI technique for a business problem
- Uninformed choice of a weak/superficial AI solution
- Lack of readiness in terms of data
- Lack of employee and/or leadership support

The growth and success of AI depend on the support and investment it receives from informed current and future organizational leaders and managers. After all, they are the sponsors, decision-makers, and end-users of AI.

To ensure its responsible and successful use and adoption, it is of utmost importance that we understand AI just as well as we understand and use applications like Microsoft Office today. This book is aimed to fill this growing skill gap in organizations. In doing so, it can provide an added competitive advantage for both short and long-term growth by teaching skills that recruiters are struggling to find in their existing workforce.

So, kudos to you for having taken on this challenge of grasping AI on a practical level. It's a technical subject, but the challenge is not as big as it may seem. Just the way you do not need to learn coding to work on a computer, you also don't have to learn to code to understand and use AI. With that in mind, this book has been structured to follow a typical AI journey you will likely face or lead.

We will start with an overview of what AI is and how you can become AI-ready. We will then visit the AI laboratory to observe the data scientists in action and understand how AI does all the different things it does. That will prepare us for the final step in our journey where, having learned which AI solution to choose for a problem and how to prepare for it, we will learn how to deploy it and get it accepted by others. We will also come to understand how AI's valuation can change as it evolves, how to formulate a corporate strategy, and how to frame a sound policy to guide its successful and responsible usage while managing the risks. Both real-world and hypothetical examples and questions will accompany us on this journey. You will also gain templates to use in every step of the process with unique frameworks such as the 7 Principles of an AI Journey©, the TUSCANE© approach, the FAB-4© model, the AI scenario analysis, AI strategy best practices, an AI valuation approach and the 7 Principles of Human-AI Work Policy©.

So, are you ready to become AI-ready? Let's begin.

Errata

We take immense pride in our work at BPB Publications and follow best practices to ensure the accuracy of our content to provide with an indulging reading experience to our subscribers. Our readers are our mirrors, and we use their inputs to reflect and improve upon human errors if any, occurred during the publishing processes involved. To let us maintain the quality and help us reach out to any readers who might be having difficulties due to any unforeseen errors, please write to us at :

errata@bpbonline.com

Your support, suggestions and feedbacks are highly appreciated by the BPB Publications' Family.

Did you know that BPB offers eBook versions of every book published, with PDF and ePub files available? You can upgrade to the eBook version at www.bpbonline.com and as a print book customer, you are entitled to a discount on the eBook copy. Get in touch with us at :

business@bpbonline.com for more details.

At **www.bpbonline.com**, you can also read a collection of free technical articles, sign up for a range of free newsletters, and receive exclusive discounts and offers on BPB books and eBooks.

BPB is searching for authors like you

If you're interested in becoming an author for BPB, please visit **www.bpbonline.com** and apply today. We have worked with thousands of developers and tech professionals, just like you, to help them share their insight with the global tech community. You can make a general application, apply for a specific hot topic that we are recruiting an author for, or submit your own idea.

The code bundle for the book is also hosted on GitHub at **https://github.com/bpbpublications/Artificial-Intelligence-for-Managers**. In case there's an update to the code, it will be updated on the existing GitHub repository.

We also have other code bundles from our rich catalog of books and videos available at **https://github.com/bpbpublications**. Check them out!

PIRACY

If you come across any illegal copies of our works in any form on the internet, we would be grateful if you would provide us with the location address or website name. Please contact us at :

business@bpbonline.com with a link to the material.

If you are interested in becoming an author

If there is a topic that you have expertise in, and you are interested in either writing or contributing to a book, please visit **www.bpbonline.com**.

REVIEWS

Please leave a review. Once you have read and used this book, why not leave a review on the site that you purchased it from? Potential readers can then see and use your unbiased opinion to make purchase decisions, we at BPB can understand what you think about our products, and our authors can see your feedback on their book. Thank you!

For more information about BPB, please visit **www.bpbonline.com**.

Table of Contents

Section - I
Beginning
an AI Journey

Welcome to Section 1 of the AI journey. We begin with an overview of why you need to learn about AI, as well as you know MS Office today. This section will provide an overview of what AI is and why it is inevitable and also risky. With unique frameworks, you will learn:

- How to make a business problem solvable by AI
- Decide whether your problem needs AI at all
- If AI is needed, how to become data ready (TUSCANE approach)
- Once ready, how to decide whether to build or buy a solution as well as what the risks are with doing AI incorrectly (FAB-4 model)

The chapters included are:

- **Chapter 1: AI Fundamentals**
- **Chapter 2: 7 Principles of an AI Journey**
- **Chapter 3: Getting Ready to use AI**

Before we dive into the depths of AI does what it does and how to use it successfully, it is important to get familiarized with the above concepts to separate myth from reality. Let's begin with the fundamentals of AI and its management.

CHAPTER 1
AI Fundamentals

We use AI every day. When Netflix recommends the next movie to watch, it is using AI. When Alexa, Siri, or Google assistant takes our commands and responds with an answer or action that is AI as well. When iPhone unlocks on seeing our face or Facebook correctly recommends the friend to tag on a picture, even that is AI.

This chapter will clear the fog around the term Artificial Intelligence. Often linked to human-like robots, AI is essentially a set of programming codes that can also be something far simpler. Let us begin by going deeper into how it works and why it is so important.

Structure

In this chapter, we will discuss the following topics:

- Definition of AI
- How AI works
- What makes AI effective?
- How AI helps us exceed our limits in solving problems?
- Growth of AI

- Machine learning and deep learning
- Data science and business intelligence
- Data science journeys

Objective

After studying this chapter, you should be able to:

- Explain the underlying logic of AI
- Understand AI's value in accomplishing tasks and solving problems
- Differentiate **artificial intelligence (AI), machine learning (ML), deep learning (DL), data science** and **business intelligence (BI)**
- Summarize how nations around the world are approaching AI
- Appreciate how the data science needs of organizations evolve

1.1 Understanding AI

Artificial Intelligence implies using a computer to do tasks the way humans would. There are many definitions out there, but essentially, it is a set of algorithms that does four things:

- Sense a given situation
- Understand it
- Take action
- Learn from the results in order to improve

Interestingly, while all AI tools follow this sequence, most are designed to give a specific output that falls in one of these categories. For example, an AI may be built to primarily do sensing - like recognizing images; or understanding - like analysing numbers; or even taking action, like recommending movies. However, it will use all these four steps to achieve that. How does all of this work?

An Algorithm is a set of tasks to be performed under specific conditions. Accordingly, an AI algorithm is programmed to take inputs, make different calculations or analyses based on those inputs and the results needed, and provide an output. However, what makes AI more advanced than a simple computer program that can also do all of this is not only the volume of information that AI can handle but its ability to learn and improve with time.

For example, let's say *Maya has a robot helper at home. Every day when she comes back from the office, the robot's task is to decide what to offer her as a beverage.* It is a simple use case but one that we will be using throughout this book to see all the different facets of AI that are potentially involved in achieving this objective.

Suppose that if Maya arrives by 7 p.m., she's happy getting a glass of water. However, if she arrives after 7 p.m., she has had a long day and prefers refreshing ice tea instead. Here, the input is time - 7 p.m., specifically. The robot is programmed to choose from two options based on the time of Maya's arrival. The output is the decision to offer water or ice tea.

Now imagine if the robot had to factor in another dimension, like the weather. If it is a hot day, cold water or ice tea may be okay, but if it is a chilly day, Maya may need room temperature water or hot tea instead.

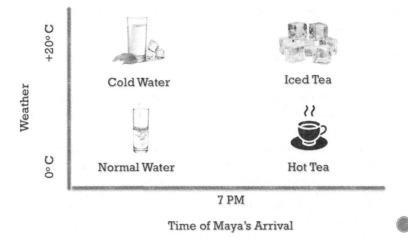

Figure 1.1: *Example of a 2-Dimensional Analysis*

We can also consider another layer of time factor. For example, Maya's behaviour may be consistent on all weekdays, except on Fridays. If Maya comes back *after 7 p.m.,* but *before 9 p.m.* on a Friday, there is a high chance that she was at work and would like ice or hot tea to drink first, just the way she normally does. But every time she comes home after 9 p.m. on a Friday, she has likely been out drinking and enjoying with friends and does not need either hot or ice tea. She instead craves water!

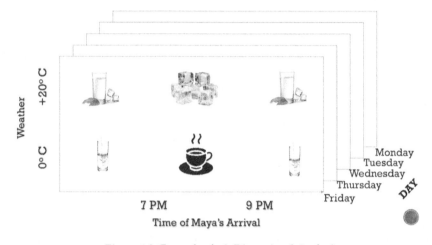

Figure 1.2: *Example of a 3-Dimensional Analysis*

We can also consider Maya's commute. On days that Maya drives a car to get back, she may not be as tired and in need of beverage as when she walks back home.

AI is important because manually, we face two limitations quite often:

- First, there is a limit to how many such factors we can consider - day, weather, time - particularly if we are not even aware of which factors there are to look at. Besides the ones we may be able to come up with that we think are important, there may be many other hidden factors or patterns influencing Maya's choice of beverage that we have no idea of.

- Second, we are also limited in our capability to analyse huge volumes of such information beyond a point. We can maybe look at what Maya drank the last 100 times she came home after 9 p.m. on a Friday in winter. But we cannot always analyse what she drank the last 1000 or 10,000 times that happened. It would be extremely time-taking to try and find the hidden patterns this way and, of course, also quite expensive. Worst of all, it may still not be very accurate.

This is why AI proves helpful. Because if the right data is available, it can do two things:

- It can quickly and inexpensively analyse what Maya likes to drink even in specific situations like when she comes home after 9 p.m. on a Friday in winter.

- It can discover the many unforeseen patterns or factors that influence Maya's choice of drink, that we haven't even thought of - such as how Maya's tastes have changed over the years, what she drank when she lived in a different city, what she drank before or after finishing school, and so on.

The underlying logic of AI – one to always keep in mind – is that there are patterns in play all around us, waiting to be found.

While we are limited in our knowledge and ability to see these patterns, AI can discover for us today what we could take years to realize. For example, would you say there is a connection between how your voice sounds and how your face looks? One wouldn't think so, but researchers at M.I.T. have created AI that can predict what you might look like based on your voice. (1). Note, however, that connections generally reveal correlations but not causations. There may be some connection between your voice and your face, but that does not necessarily mean that one is the result of the other.

A more common example would be that of big retailers that are always trying to analyse their customers' buying behaviour in order to send them coupons and offers that they may be interested in. You may recall the story about how Target figured out that a girl was pregnant even before her father did! (2). While that story may not have been entirely accurate (3) it serves as a great example of understanding the potential of AI. For instance, the AI in question here was claimed to have uncovered a pattern where sometime in the first 20 weeks, pregnant women loaded up on supplements like calcium, magnesium, and zinc. Allegedly, women on the baby registry were also buying large quantities of unscented lotion at the beginning of their second trimester. Finding such hidden patterns and insights is where AI beats a simpler analysis. It matters because the very survival and evolutionary success of humans over other species has been due to our ability to recognize patterns in the world around us and to estimate what is happening or is likely to happen in a given situation.

1.2 Growth of AI

AI is so much more than just robots. It is growing fast because it can handle large amounts of hidden or new data quickly and can therefore take care of a lot of mundane things, freeing up all that time for us to make decisions and get results. The lesser time we spend analysing what time and day it is, what the weather is like, and so on, the quicker we can get down to serving Maya water or tea. What is also boosting our need for AI is our declining cognitive ability: the more we use phones and other digital technologies, the more distracted we become. It sounds like a chicken-and-egg story! As humans, our ability to focus has now reduced to less than eight seconds. Believe it or not, that's less than that of a goldfish. (4).

AI is also timing itself well to converge neatly with Blockchain and the **Internet of Things (IoT).** An article I came across summarized the impact of this convergence nicely: Blockchain can build secure networks and unending trails of data from which AI can extract meaningful information to enable intelligent IoT systems to perform their actions in an efficient and reliable way! (5).

AI has started to be used aggressively by companies globally and is at the forefront of government policies. It was expected to boost profitability by 38% by 2035, according to an Accenture report (6), and would have added over 15.7 trillion dollars to the global GDP by 2030, according to PWC. (7). The growth was underlined in 2017 by Russian President Vladimir Putin, who said that whoever becomes the leader in AI will become the ruler of the world. It was soon followed by SpaceX and Tesla CEO Elon Musk, who added that competition in AI security at the national level would most likely be the cause of WW3. (8).

No surprise then that 2017 and 2018 saw governments worldwide quickly come up with their own viewpoint and strategic plan around AI, with policies to govern it, thereby officially setting off a race towards AI leadership. You can find a great summary infographic on the global state of AI shared by Tim Dutton on the Medium platform in an article titled *An Overview of National AI Strategies. (9).*

The question is: how do we use AI in the right way? For instance, China has been using it to calculate the Social Score of its citizens, where the machine decides correct and incorrect behaviour by continuously collecting all data on an individual and following the four steps of AI analysis discussed earlier. As a result, you get points for paying your bills on time, being socially involved, or even stopping at a red light! With higher social scores, you can get social benefits like faster application processing and even priority on dating apps! (10). All of this, though, requires more advanced AI techniques. For instance, the red-light behaviour tracking is managed by cameras installed at every intersection to capture and recognize your face. That is the domain of deep learning. In order to get to that, let's first understand why you have to talk about something called machine learning today and not artificial intelligence, if you want to be taken seriously.

1.3 AI versus ML versus DL versus data science vs. BI

In this segment, we will come up to speed with how advanced AI is today. We learned that artificial intelligence algorithms receive inputs, analyze them based on pre-set rules, and give an output accordingly. It requires any AI algorithm to be specifically told how to analyze the information it gets and to take action. There are rules that have been specified to guide how AI runs its analysis. However, AI can also be programmed to figure out the analysis on its own. Machine learning is this self-learning form of AI, which looks at all the different inputs in a situation historically and then looks at what their consequent outputs were. It then tries to map these two to develop its own understanding of how a set of inputs led to a certain output. This difference between self-learning and rule-based learning approach makes all the difference in AI becoming *intelligent*:

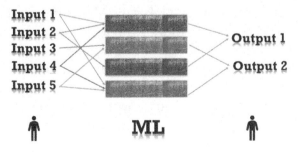

Figure 1.3: Overview of machine learning

In the case of Maya, her robot would first look at the beverage she drank every working day over the last year and the corresponding conditions that prevailed that day. In the first instance, it would see that water was served only if she arrived before 7 p.m. It would also come across those occasional Fridays when Maya had water each time she arrived after 9 p.m. It would look at the difference in water temperature served in winter months vs. summer months, and so on. In other words, the robot would teach itself how to decide which beverage to serve Maya, and because it would look at many more factors than just the time, day or weather, it would start to be more and more accurate in its decision with every passing day. That is machine learning.

We will learn about the popular machine learning techniques later in this course to see the various ways it can work in. But even machine learning has its limitations and cannot accurately mimic human levels of analysis. For instance, the robot may learn what to serve Maya based on whether her diet for the day indicates that she has a cold, but how will it decide what to serve based on her mood? For that, at the very least, the robot would have to be able to interpret the many expressions on Maya's face, deduce her tone of speech, and so on. This is where deep learning comes into the picture.

DL is an advanced form of machine learning that can run a quick analysis of huge amounts of data to a level that would be too much, even for ordinary machine learning to handle on its own. If machine learning is the latest buzzword, deep learning is definitely the new sexy. After all, the winners of the 2018 Turing award - considered the Nobel Prize for computing - were all champions of this field. DL is the closest that AI has so far come to working like a human, because it copies the way our brain processes information with the use of neural networks. That is what it takes for AI to differentiate between a dog and a wolf, even though they can look similar at times; or to recognize your face whether you laugh, cry or remain solemn. That is also what it takes AI to try an entirely new approach to develop an antibiotic that can kill even antibiotic-resistant bacteria! (11). We will process DL in further detail in its own dedicated chapter because there's so much to learn.

Before we conclude this chapter, a quick word on data science and **business intelligence (BI),** you may have heard about these terms often. Data science refers to the processing and analysis of data to get insights, which may involve simple mathematics, statistics, pattern recognition, data management, or other techniques, including but not necessarily, artificial intelligence. Business intelligence, on the other hand, deals with visualizing current and past information on dashboards for reporting, and manual or even AI-based analysis. In a way, BI shows the past that we can use to estimate the future, whereas AI analyses that past to give an output, take action, or even predict the future:

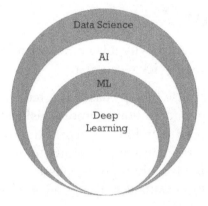

Figure 1.4: Layers of Data Science

Perhaps an ideal way to summarize the analytical journey – from data collection to Deep Learning – is the *Data Science Hierarchy of Needs* from an article by *Monica Rogati, (12)* built-in line with the famous Maslow's Hierarchy of Needs for humans. It delineates the order in which data and processes have to be in place for AI success. Accordingly, organizations generally move from a need to collect data (through sensors, logging, user generation, and so on) to moving or storing them in the right place. The latter involves pipelines, proper infrastructure, and data flow management.

With data properly accessible, they can now explore, and if required, transform it. It implies finding anomalies and outliers, cleaning the data, and readying it for analysis. It leads to the next stage of aggregating or labelling the data with a focus on specific analytical insights and metrics, as well as to train the AI model, as we will see later. Organizations are generally ready to learn from analysis of the data by this stage, but start small with experimentation and simple AI algorithms.

These are all the stages that organizations invariably go through before finally arriving at the top of the hierarchy, where they are now positioned to employ full-scale advanced AI techniques like DL. The quicker an organization reaches the top, the better its growth prospects and competitive readiness are. It's time to see how we can achieve that.

Conclusion

We now know what AI is, why it is important, and how advanced it currently is. Let's do a quick recap first.

AI is important because it helps tackle our reduced ability to focus, the sheer volume of information to process, rising costs, and a lack of time that we are faced with today. It works through essentially four steps: it senses information with its ability to ingest a high volume of inputs, understands it through various forms of analysis, takes an action as per the resultant output, and improves over time by learning and adapting to newer data.

The self-learning ability to decipher patterns simply by looking at inputs and their corresponding outputs allows AI to morph into ML. And if ML can ingest significantly large sets of information and process them the way a human brain does, it has graduated to DL. All of these are elements of the field of Data Science, which also constitutes simply visualizing information to make sense of it, better called BI.

While BI looks at the past and presents it in an easy-to-understand manner to help us understand what's happened or estimate what may happen, AI analyses the past to give us a deeper – and otherwise invisible – understanding of what happened and help predict the future more accurately.

Data science journeys evolve over time - from a focus on collecting data, to moving or storing them in the right place, to exploring or transforming them as per an organization's needs and processes. The next stage is often to aggregate and prepare them for deeper analysis, followed by the actual AI analysis to lend deep actionable insights.

As we can see, the journey to AI success involves layers of managerial assessment around a team's readiness and the development of a core solution. Different organizations find themselves at different stages of this journey. Therefore, understanding AI's components and requirements, and pursuing it in a systematic manner, is crucial to help prevent teams from jumping on to AI usage without being ready first: a common reason why AI investments tend to fail.

It is now time to start the AI journey aimed to see how organizations can go about solving a given business problem. The first step is to understand some of the basic managerial principles to always keep in mind. That will be our focus next.

Questions

1. Which of these are benefits of AI?
    A. It can reduce costs
    B. It can do a job quicker
    C. It can reveal hidden insights
    D. All of the above.

2. Which of the following are potential AI use cases and which are BI use cases:
    I.   I want to see which months in the year I usually sell more
    II. I want to predict my revenues for the next 6 months
    III. I want to identify the technical skills or background information that indicate a high chance of success in an employee in my company
    IV. I want to identify the technical skills or background information that my highest performing employees have had

    A. II & III require AI. I & IV can be solved by BI
    B. All require AI

     C. All can be solved by BI

     D. I can be solved by BI. II, III & IV require AI.

3. The underlying logic of AI is that there are .... in play all around us, waiting to be found. It typically does 4 things to achieve that: Sense, Understand, Take Action, and   .

4. An .... is a set of tasks to be performed under specific conditions.

5. Is this statement true or false? Machine Learning differs from basic AI in that it automates the middle process of analysis to see how certain inputs led to a certain output.

Answers

1. D

2. A

   Explanation: II & III require predicting the future or unknown information, and will require AI. I & IV require simply visualizing what has happened in the past.

3. Patterns, Learn

4. Algorithm

5. True

CHAPTER 2

7 Principles of an AI Journey

We learned about the difference between BI and AI. How does one journey from one to the other? While BI can show us business trends and patterns in data, it normally takes manual labor to analyze those visuals to get actionable insights that one can act on. The latter can be automated with AI. Generally, organizations use AI solutions to analyze and reveal insights which they visualize using a BI layer. It is perhaps why the focus, effort, and investment of companies, in general, has evolved over the last years like clockwork - from statistical analysis to BI usage to data readiness for advanced analysis, to finally, AI.

The jump to AI always involves certain basic truths that we should always keep in mind, and that separates it from regular analytics. We now look at the principles that should guide any AI journey.

Structure

In this chapter, we will discuss the following topics:

- A real-life example of beginning an AI journey
- Problem framing for AI

- Fit and readiness elements of AI journeys
- Blackbox AI
- Seven principles of AI journeys

Objective

After studying this chapter, you should be able to:

- Appreciate the components involved in the decision-making around AI
- Understand what makes AI-based decisions risky
- Differentiate AI's definition of a *problem* from a business problem
- Understand the importance of determining fit and readiness for AI
- Decipher the adoption issues and usage objectives to consider in AI
- Realize that AI may not always be the best solution

2.1 The big problem

We have seen some stellar examples of successful AI journeys, most of which occur in the technology space unsurprisingly. A great example would that of Hitachi, which uses machine learning in amazing ways – from fighting cyberbullying to making decisions based on demand fluctuations. It announced H in 2015, which could be applied to several applications rather than being useful for only specific ones. It has proven efficient in screening urine samples to detect cancer, monitor and combat food waste in hospitals, reduce emission levels to improve a ship's fuel efficiency, and even detect fraud or make accurate forecasts for businesses. (1).

Hitachi's H is a rare case, though. Most AI solutions are generally best when they are built and used for specific purposes. Unfortunately, too many organizations buy an AI solution, and then try to decide which problems to solve with it. It is why organizations fail to get value out of even good AI solutions. That is not the only roadblock, though. Besides data issues, which we will discuss later, and a lack of specialists, a lack of business alignment and understanding of AI among non-technical employees are as much to blame. A company culture not appreciating the need for AI was the number one reason for slow AI adoption in a 2019 survey report. (2).

Avoiding disillusionment with AI depends as much on the managers as it does on the data scientists. After all, while it is the job of data scientists and engineers to build a working AI model, it is the manager's job to see it used successfully. A successful AI journey will bring the leader out of you. What better way to put this in context than to look at a real-life example. So, let me start with how I adopted AI in one of my organizations.

The big problem my team faced was on the sales side: how to win new customers. Our organization had decided to reposition itself, and we now wanted to target a new specific audience group. We achieved it using four tools, only two of which were AI-enabled, even though all four could be:

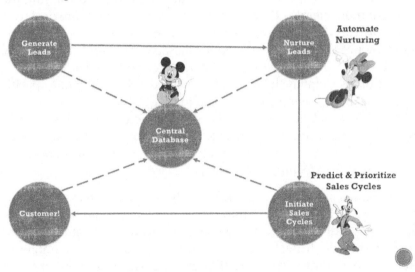

Figure 2.1: *A technology stack overview*

2.2 Initiating an AI journey

Our first step was to break down the big problem statement into individual steps that are involved on the sales side. We nurture a list of prospects called leads, which can come from various sources, including unknown people who find us online. Once leads show interest in our product and are willing to talk about it, we start a sales cycle with them where the team chases those leads to convert them into paying customers. All of this information on leads and sales cycles are stored in a database on our CRM software. It was our base platform. Let's call it Mickey. Being a central repository of all our sales data, the first thing for us to keep in mind was that any new software we use or that we bring in should be able to feed data into Mickey, to make sure that all our data stays in one place. And that is **Lesson One**. Organizations usually end up having silos where different teams or functions have their data in different systems. *Try to bring all your data into one system or at least connect them to one in order to allow a seamless flow of information.*

Lesson Two: *As mentioned above, the first step in approaching AI use is to break down the core problem that you're trying to solve into specific use cases. That means breaking that big statement - 'winning more customers' - into more specific tasks that need to be accomplished to achieve it.* To do this, you have to spend some time understanding and framing the problem more clearly. It's important because AI models are designed to perform tasks, and there may be several involved in solving a single problem, not all of which may be addressable by a single AI solution. It is the big difference between 'Narrow AI' and 'General AI.' Most AI around us today is the former type: good at handling one specific task. What most business leaders and managers assume AI to be is the latter – Artificial General Intelligence, which refers to AI that can one day cope with any generalized task as humans can. Consequently, problem framing is where the bulk of miscommunication between the business and technical teams takes place.

For our small sales team to spend their limited time on chasing leads that are most likely to turn into customers, we needed to automate the first half of the sales process leading up to those qualified and interested leads. It deals with nurturing the leads to gauge interest and would require a software that could perform a range of tasks: send out emails to thousands of prospects, remain compliant with the anti-spam laws, follow those up with emails that are being sent periodically, and alert the team when a phone call or another channel of contact could be helpful, say, after every five attempts. It would also need to update all information and lead status on Mickey - our central database. These steps did not necessarily require a powerful machine learning solution. What mandated it was the need to keep track of all the responses we would get as a result of these reach outs. To automate even that to some extent, we needed software that could also read and interpret the replies to deduce whether it was positive, negative or an out-of-office response. That required a more robust technique, likely a natural language processing capability - NLP.

We will learn about NLP later in this course when we cover the different AI techniques. For now, it serves as a great example of how understanding the different techniques, even on a higher level, can be so helpful. It allows us to quickly estimate which techniques may help, and which would likely not, once we have broken a big problem into a specific task we are trying to address. It then allows us to quickly qualify or disqualify the many software options available, given our existing resources and limitations and the relative strength of the techniques and approach used by different solutions. It is important because, in a real-life scenario, we do not always have time to look at every possible solution in the market.

Our search narrowed the options down to three vendors. Each could send 1-to-1 emails and follow-ups, read and categorize responses, and update all the information into our central database on Mickey. One of them was also quite popular and proven. However, there was a relatively new and lesser-known solution in the market with decent reviews that could also learn progressively to determine when to send a follow-up email to different leads based on the highest likelihood of getting a response from each of them. That takes more than just NLP, and that was our choice. Let's call the software Minnie.

*Minnie wasn't the most popular software out there but it was the right fit for our needs. That is **Lesson Three**.*

2.3 Influencing the AI effectiveness

With the list of interested leads identified regularly and updated on Mickey, our team could start chasing the resultant sales cycles. However, with hundreds of shortlisted leads with varying degrees of genuine interest - some interested, others not so much - the salespeople could still spend their time chasing a lot of cycles that looked good on paper but were not. The AI software could have been wrong in estimating a lead's interest. Even the salespeople can often get biased by how nicely a customer spoke to them, how big the potential revenue is, and so on. Moreover, winning a deal depends as much on the sellers' behavior as on customer interest. It depends on their compliance with proven sales best practices and operational requirements in place, as well as the custom conditions faced in a given opportunity. What we needed now was some guidance on how to prioritize further the sales cycles, based on how likely they were to result in a won deal. It needed software that could make intelligent predictions based on a host of tangible and not-so-tangible factors. We chose to go for Goofy here.

Goofy was a surprisingly intuitive yet inexpensive software that took over the moment active sales cycles began on Mickey for a given lead. It could predict which opportunities were likely to close in a given period by analyzing all our sales history data on Mickey so that our team could prioritize the more important ones first. What stole the show was Goofy's ability to explain the rationale behind its predictions. In the face of all known and unknown factors being analyzed, it clearly showed which ones it had looked at, and how, to judge and predict the sales deals. Given this transparency, salespeople were able to make contextual decisions on whether an AI recommendation was relevant or not, and when to listen to it and when not to. That is **Lesson Four:** *As far as feasible, opt for AI solutions that are not black box, and can explain the rationale behind their insights.*

As a neat little add-on, Goofy also showed us where data was missing in our data set in real-time so that we could make sure the dataset was in proper shape for the AI to give us accurate insights. That was a boon. Because AI is only as good as the data, it analyses, ensuring that the data is ready is crucial for any company using AI. *And that can also involve setting up a process for employees that are responsible for entering or updating data.* That is **Lesson Five**. We will discuss this in detail in the next chapter.

Another great thing about Minnie and Goofy was that both were simple to use, thereby not requiring a steep learning curve for the employees to start using them. It helped with adoption. *Effectiveness of any AI tool in an organization is determined by how easily and how well it is being used, its direct impact on business results, and its collateral impact on existing systems and resources in place. The latter should generally be minimal.* That is **Lesson Six**.

Any tool you pick should fit into your operational process and work with the other software in tandem to create a proper flow of information. You don't want a new AI software to come in and disrupt everything that's already existing in the organization. We set up certain metrics around each tool and its usage, such as the proportion of interesting leads converting into customers, reduction in the length of our annual sales cycles, percentage of data completeness, etc. In the end, we had managed to engage 10x more customers while reducing the operational cost by 15%.

Finally, **Lesson Seven:** *Not everything has to be AI.* Consider Deep Learning, which can be costly, complex, and requires a lot of authentic and accurate data. It may not always be worth the effort to use one for a business problem. Or consider the case of a business that has recently undergone a change in its model or entered a new sector. Data that belonged to the old model or sector may not be relevant for any machine learning solution tasked to analyze the new business model or sector. Even Mickey could be AI-enabled. The fourth software in our stock, which we haven't discussed, was not AI because with Minnie and Goofy doing their jobs, the fourth software's job was quite simple. All it had to do was score anti-spam compliant website visitors based on their activity and add them to the lead list that Minnie was sending e-mails to. Yes, there is software that can do such lead scoring while also doing other wonderful things with AI. Still, our software sale was heavily dependent on a consultative qualifying process and thus relied on direct missionary sale. For us, the fourth software was an opportunity to reduce cost and training effort.

As you can see, there were several components involved in this chain of decision making around AI enablement. Let us now break these down into simple pillars that will guide you to get started with AI too successfully.

Conclusion

Seven principles should always be kept in mind while adopting AI:

1. Have all data in one place or have them seamlessly connected to one system.

2. As a first step, break down the core problem into specific use cases that may or may not be solved by AI.

3. Choose the software that's the right fit for your needs, budget & existing organizational systems and processes, rather than going for the most popular ones.

4. Choose AI software that can show the rationale behind its analysis, especially for critical tasks and decision making.

5. Ensure that data is proper and ready for AI use.

6. Effective AI requires proper adoption by the users, the right processes to support it, the right measures to keep it working properly, and only the desired degree of disruption to existing systems and processes.

7. Not all solutions have to be AI.

These principles are designed to aid the preparation for AI use and ensuring its effectiveness. Principle #5 refers to *proper data*, while Principles #2, #3, and #7 correspond to the choice of AI solution to solve a business problem. What do these entail? The next chapter takes us into the specific of how to become AI-ready.

Questions

1. Is this statement true or false? Most organizations use BI to derive insights and visualize them for ease of interpretation on an AI layer.

2. Is this statement true or false? Not everything has to be AI, but if we decide to use AI, we should focus on how well it fits with our needs, budget, and processes in place.

3. Even with the right fit, the effectiveness of any AI tool in an organization is determined by which of the following:

    I.   How well it is used in the organization

    II. How proper the data being fed into it is

    III. How well it can completely replace old systems

    IV. How well it is accepted by the users

    A. I, II & IV
    B. I, II & III
    C. II, III & IV
    D. All of them

4. As far as feasible, we should opt for AI solutions that are not .... so that they can explain the rationale behind their insights. We should also ensure that all .... is in one place system or is well connected to allow an uninterrupted flow of information.

5. Is this statement true or false? Since there are AI solutions in the market that can handle multiple use cases, we do not always need to break down the core problem into specific use cases.

Answers

1. False

2. True

3. A

   Explanation: A good AI tool does not always have to replace the old systems in place. Prevalent systems can be helpful, and replacing them can cause unnecessary disruption and unrest in the organization.

4. Black Box, Data

5. False

CHAPTER 3
Getting Ready to Use AI

Choosing the right set of software is about managing the cost-benefit ratio. The decision an organization is trying to make is whether it needs AI at all and whether to build or buy a solution. Either option should be a possible fit with the realities of the organization. After all, Maya would not want a robot that either does not work with her other home automation installations or does things that others already manage well. She may also find that it is far simpler to get water or tea herself than to train and get a robot to do it for her. Let us now look at what good data looks like, how we become data ready, and how it is used in AI modeling.

Structure

In this chapter, we will discuss the following topics:

- The TUSCANE approach
- Data dictionary
- RACI Framework
- Data preprocessing in AI modeling

- Importance of problem framing for AI
- FAB-4 model

Objective

After studying this chapter, you should be able to:

- Understand the components of good data that is AI-ready
- Map the data, processes and KPI's in place, and identify gaps
- Understand how data is treated in any AI modeling
- Break down problems into use cases that can be solved by AI
- Find the right AI solution for your use case

3.1 Becoming data ready

A crucial determinant of the above decision and a crucial factor behind AI functioning well is Data. A 2019 report mentioned that 96% of organizations ran into problems with AI and machine learning projects, primarily owing to data. (1). A few years back, the Chairman and CEO at Caterpillar had suggested that they were losing $9 - $18 billion in easy sales revenue as their sales weren't monetizing the real value of data. (2). The availability of the right data depends on the processes that are already in place to capture it, as well as employee diligence in keeping that data up to date. An algorithm can make incorrect predictions or analysis for a host of reasons, not the least because the data we fed into it was erroneous or insufficient in some way. Consider a hypothetical scenario where Maya may have collected thousands of digital photos in PNG format to feed into her robot so that it can analyze them and learn to recognize her face in the future. However, she finds that the robot accepts photos only in JPG format. Maya would now face an arduous task of converting thousands of photos into the right format for the robot to understand it. She may also find that she simply does not have enough photos to train the robot properly.

3.1.1 The TUSCANE approach

The data required for an AI solution should always fulfill a set of conditions. For ease of remembering, let's call these conditions TUSCANE, rhyming with *Tuscany*. Anything Tuscan is perfect like the region's finesse, but what does *perfect* mean here?

Any data should be **Timely**, which means that it is either up to date, getting updated regularly, or belonging to the time that is being analyzed. A classic example would be the Covid19 pandemic, which changed business behavior, thereby making a lot of data on previous business models unfit to use anymore.

It should be **Usable**, which generally requires data to be in one place and available without restrictions so that it can be easily accessed. For example, we cannot use customers' data even if it is available, without their explicit permission.

The data should be **Structured**. Most AI solutions a business manager will likely come across today will require structured data. However, strictly in data science parlance, AI can also work with unstructured data. For a business manager, 'structure' implies a dataset that is not effectively garbage and devoid of logic, relevance, or analysability to the problem that AI is supposed to solve.

Data should be **Complete**. Incomplete data has to be dealt with and filled out for AI to properly analyze information, as we will discuss in the chapter on AI modeling.

It should also be **Accurate**. Inaccurate or erroneous data is the number one reason for inaccurate results.

Data should also be **Neutral** and not biased. The number two reason for inaccurate results and the number one reason to think about AI ethics is bias. Bias in data is often difficult to catch and can lead to insights that appear accurate at first but cease to be if the situation changes. Worse, the insights may continue to appear accurate even if they are not. For example, if AI were asked today to determine who has a higher earning potential between men or women based on historical data, it would likely choose the former simply because men in most cultures have historically been the bread earners in the household. It would be the wrong conclusion.

Finally, data should also be **Enough**. As we will learn in Section 3, techniques like Deep Learning or even Machine Learning require a lot of data to be effective. We must possess enough volume of data to train an AI model properly.

3.1.2 Data Dictionary

So, how do you become data ready? A great best place to start is first to get a data dictionary in place. It can be a simple excel file or record but helps expose any gaps in an organization's knowledge and control over its data. A data dictionary typically contains information on three fronts:

- Data details, which lends information needed to access or make any changes to the data itself
- Processes, which the data is part of and which are used to collect or use the data
- KPIs, or the primary measures that the business tracks to make sense of the organizational data and performance

For each data field recorded or relevant for the organization, the accompanying information can include, but is not limited to:

- How and for what processes or use case is the data being used?
- Who are the process owners and stakeholders?
- What are the focus KPIs in place?
- What are the data inputs involved in those KPIs?
- Data attributes, that is, the data format, size, and other such information
- Where each type of data resides
- Who is the owner or person/department responsible?
- Where is it sourced from, and how frequently?
- The TUSCANE validity of data
- Any accompanying issues with data (for example, data integrity could be suspect)

The data dictionary normally belongs to a CIO and is managed by his/her IT team responsible for the data and technology assets and stack management across the organization. A proven framework that can help manage the data dictionary is **RACI**, which helps record who is **responsible**, who is **accountable**, who needs to be **consulted**, and who needs to be kept **informed** on a given process and developments. (3). Without it, it is alarming to see how often organizations miss the beat in getting a good handle on the process of procuring, securing, and maintaining both the data and the technology stack in the house. So, if you find an organization missing a data dictionary, which is often the case, you know where to start leading its AI journey.

3.1.3 Data Preprocessing

We come now to the use of data in AI modeling. Data scientists have to treat the data in five ways to get it ready for any model. First is **Labelling**. The data may have to be labeled, depending on the kind of techniques being used. Most machine learning solutions require at least the independent and dependent variables to be specified, for instance. What are these? If Maya's choice of the drink depends on her time of arrival at home, the drink is the 'dependent' variable while her time of arrival is the independent variable.

Second is **Completeness**. As we just learned, all missing fields of data in a dataset must first be taken care of. There are ways to do this. For example, if the weather information on certain days when Maya came back home last year is missing, we can fill that information on any given day simply by taking the average of the previous day and the next day's weather.

The third is **Encoding**. Particularly in the case of categorical data, it must be encoded at times into a continuous numerical format for ease of computation. Categorical data refers to data that is not a continuous value (for example, numbers like 1, 2, 3, and so on); instead, it is a distinct category (for example, type of drinks like tea, water, coffee, and so on). So, in Maya's dataset, we would likely have to denote 'tea' by the number 0 and 'water' by the number 1, to use it in the same equation as the weather, which is a number.

Fourth and quite important is **Feature Scaling**. Even if different variables are in number format, they may have a wildly different scale of values. For example, while the weather may range from 0°C to 30°C, Maya's monthly expenditure on groceries may range from $200 to $500. If the grocery expense is also an important factor to be considered in determining the choice of tea or water, the model may end up getting biased towards these larger numbers - 200 and 500—as compared to the smaller digits like 0 and 30 (degrees). It is why feature scaling is important as it helps balance the comparison.

Finally, we have a **Split**. The data set is split into a training set and a test set for the machine to train on a portion of data and then test its conclusions with the actual results on the remaining data. We will see this in detail in the chapter on AI modeling.

So always ask yourself and the team: Are you ready with data? And if not, can you be ready fairly easily to use it without delay? Often, organizations will find themselves fixing data issues after they have invested in AI. True, machine learning solutions can often demand their data treatment. However, that is also why the best practice is first to get the house in order when it comes to data. Otherwise, it can be a highly inefficient use of resources to get the data sorted in a silo specifically for one solution, and then again for another. Anticipating that an organization will utilize more and more AI sooner or later, getting the data and accompanying processes in shape is a good first step.

Let us now distill our focus down from general data readiness to the specific problem at hand that we would like to solve. The question is whether it makes sense to explore AI solutions to solve that business problem at all, and if so, whether to build or buy one.

3.2 Choosing the right solution

Not all problems require AI, and not all problems can be best solved using AI. Too many companies decide to use AI software—Machine learning, mostly—and then go looking for the best way to use it. Most often than not, they find that they are not ready to get results from the software.

As mentioned before, the right way is to begin by first asking and clearly defining what problem it is that we are trying to solve. Break that problem down to specific use cases or tasks that one or more software would be able to perform. In the case of Maya's robot, the problem is to serve Maya the right drink. Of all the things the robot needs to do to achieve this, one is to predict whether Maya will have tea or water. That's a use case.

The question that follows next is: Is that the right use case or set of use cases for machine learning, given what the technology is capable of doing or not doing? Machine learning may not be the right fit for a host of reasons - lack of capability to solve a particular problem, lack of readiness on the part of the organization, the time and costs involved in comparison to non-AI alternatives, and so on.

If we are to use AI, we need to decide whether to build a machine learning solution in-house or to buy a readymade software outside. Both these questions are often best understood by looking at the available software options in the market. Why is that? It's because it is quicker to refer to what already exists, and a great way for us to understand how a given problem is currently being solved and what it requires. A good way to start the search is to think about what kind of output you're looking for from any solution and the kind of techniques that may help accordingly. As we will see in *Section 3*, different techniques yield different kinds of outputs. In the case of Maya, our task is to make a prediction, and the result we want is a discrete category: water or tea. So, any technique that cannot make predictions, or whose output is not definite but a constant value (for example, numbers) may not be helpful. It helps shortlist our options.

3.2.1 The FAB-4 model

With the use case and the output type clear, we follow something called the Fab-4 model. **FAB** stands for **Find, Answer** and **Build**. Each of these three phases consists of four components. Hence, FAB-Four.

In the following figure, notice on the right side that six software options in the market were being considered in the beginning. Their outputs were either numerical or categorical. Let's say that the output we are looking for in our use case is a category (tea or water). So, solutions 1, 3, and 6 are out. Now, how do we choose between options 2, 4, and 5? And given these shortlisted options, would it be better to build a solution in-house simply?

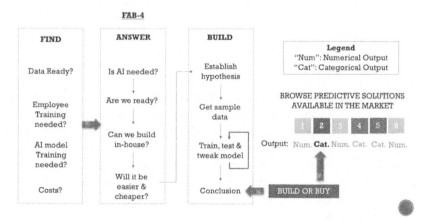

Figure 3.1: FAB-4 Model

The first step – FIND—helps shortlist further from these remaining options in the market. Here you'll be looking for four things in your shortlisted options:

1. Do you have the data the software requires, as we saw earlier?

2. How much training will employees need to go through to use the software?

3. How much training and time does the software itself need to show results?

4. The cost of the software, including hidden resource costs if it will hinder other software and processes in the organization

Once you have considered these, you will have a good idea of what the most suitable software option in the market can be for your problem, or how the use case is being addressed by others. The next step – ANSWER—refers to finalizing between buying the shortlisted solution or building one in-house. It involves answering the following four questions.

1. Given the options seen in the market and the realities of the organization, is AI necessarily the most effective choice for the problem? We will learn more about the cost-benefit analysis in *Section 4*.

2. If the solution does need AI, is your organization set up to use it in terms of data, capabilities, employees, and processes?

3. If your organization is ready, should you get the software immediately or can you wait to build software in-house, and will that put you at a competitive disadvantage?

4. If you can wait, given your organization's current in-house expertise, will it be easier and cheaper to build a similar or better software than buying the shortlisted one available in the market?

Answers to these questions can allow clarity on the solution to go ahead with. Whether you decide to explore building a solution in-house or buying one through a third-party vendor, you will likely have to oversee the core steps—either from scratch or in customizing the software. The next step – BUILD—elucidates these. The intensity of work in this stage may vary, but the conclusion should make it clear early enough whether you are on the right path, or need to adjust strategies.

1. Start by establishing a hypothesis that you will try to prove or disprove with your machine learning model. In our case, let's say the hypothesis is that Maya would like tea.

2. Get the appropriate sample data to run an effective analysis.

3. Build, train, and test that AI model on this data to check your hypothesis. We will see how this is done by the data scientists in the next section.

4. Analyze the results to conclude whether the current machine learning model is effective, indeed.

If required, you can refine your hypothesis, tweak the model, and repeat this process until you get satisfactory results to make a decision. However, if you try to force a machine learning solution on the wrong problem or in the wrong conditions, you can go on in circles tweaking the model and data to get results, to no end. As should be apparent, you don't want to go through this cyclical process to determine whether a given solution or AI, in general, is more useful than any other method, and whether to build or buy one.

3.2.2 Other issues to consider

We should watch out for the hidden costs. Most teams may decide to buy an AI solution, as few can afford a robust team of quality data scientists and engineers. However, the solution can often require significant customization of the model by the third-party vendor for your specific business and data realities, which may not be visible at first.

While some things are too simple to require AI, some may be too difficult. For example, AI can identify correlations but not causations. Let's say Maya's robot correctly identified that every 12 weeks, Maya's tea consumption goes up for a week. However, it may not be able to decipher why that was the case. That said, scientists are now trying to address this issue (4) by teaching machines to understand why. (5). If AI does start to understand what causes something to happen, it will have become intelligent indeed.

Another issue for machine learning is in detecting anomalies, although good machine learning solutions are designed to get rid of these on their own. For instance, while the robot may identify regular spikes in Maya's consumption of tea, it will have a far bigger problem taking these spikes into account if they were truly random and outside any identifiable pattern.

These steps should have offered clarity on why so many AI onboarding initiatives in companies tend to yield lower results today. The next step is to worry about the deployment and implementation process of a chosen AI solution in the organization. But first, we have to make sure we have chosen the right solution to deploy. To achieve that, we must understand the different types of AI techniques and the problems they help solve. It's now time to learn how AI does some of the amazing things it does.

Conclusion

Data readiness and the choice of the right AI (or non-AI) solution is crucial before undertaking any AI journey. The templates shared in this chapter can aid the process for us. In summary, there are three aspects to keep in mind in terms of data readiness:

- *Is the data ready for AI?* The TUSCANE approach is a handy checklist to check whether the data is timely, usable, structured, complete, accurate, not biased, and enough in volume.

- *How to get the data ready and maintain it that way?* Whether or not the current data meets our requirements, it is important to put a data dictionary in place to track the data, associated processes and KPI's, and to surface any gaps therein. It includes clearly outlining the individuals responsible, accountable, and to be consulted and kept informed.

- *What happens to the data in AI modeling?* All data has to be preprocessed for an AI model before building the solution. The steps normally require ensuring the right labeling, completeness, encoding, and feature scaling. Data is also split between a set that the AI model is trained on and another that it is tested on. We cover this in later chapters.

The choice of an AI solution relies on a suitable breakdown of a business problem into specific use cases. Remember that we mostly encounter Narrow AI around us, which, unlike General AI, is aimed for specific tasks. For a given use case(s), we have to address some questions to find potential solutions, finalize one to go ahead with, and build or customize it to suit our specific needs. The FAB-4 model can help us quickly check if we may be going down a wrong path to minimize any loss of investments, which could be due to our lack of readiness or the limitations machine learning itself faces in what it can do.

FAB-4 kicks in once a problem have been broken down for machine learning. It allows us to find potential solutions, assesses their fit, and then builds or buy and customize a solution that meets our specific organizational requirement. Find, Answer, and Build can together allow us to pick an option and validate quickly whether it is the right choice.

FAB-4 brings us to the doorstep of AI techniques. It banks on us having some idea of which techniques are likely to offer a solution to our problem use case. Time to understand, conceptually, the major AI techniques.

Questions

1. Order the following steps involved in approaching the best solution to solve a problem using machine learning?

   I. Determine if it would be cheaper, easier, quicker and better performance-wise to buy or build a Machine Learning solution in-house

   II. Find the best available Machine Learning solution in the market for one or more tasks

   III. Get the data ready to be used by the chosen Machine Learning solution

   IV. Clearly understand the problem and identify the tasks required to solve it

   V. Identify how much and how good the data you have is, to use Machine Learning well

   A. I > V > IV > II > III
   B. IV > II > I > V > III
   C. IV > V > II > I > III
   D. IV > V > II > III > I

2. I have checked my data. It is timely, usable, structured, complete, accurate, and enough in volume to be used by my chosen Machine Learning solution. Could there still be something wrong with the data?

   A. Yes
   B. No
   C. Only if the chosen solution has other specific requirements

3. A data dictionary is a useful starting step to get the data in order. Also, it helps manage the .... and KPIs relevant to a business.

4. We should be careful when interpreting insights from AI not to confuse correlations between two variables with .... ?

5. Is this statement True or False? If we don't first ensure that an AI solution is helpful for a given business problem and that our data and process are ready to leverage it, we risk going in circles in trying to tweak the model and get results from the solution.

Answers

1. C

   Explanation: Keep in mind that many times, data readiness depends on the machine learning solution being considered. Many solutions source their data.

2. A

   Explanation: The data may be biased, which will result in a biased output.

3. Process

4. Causation

5. True

Section - II
Choosing the Right AI Techniques

Welcome to Section 2 of the AI journey. In this section, we will enter the AI laboratory to look at how and where AI models are created. We will also look at the different AI techniques without becoming too technical. This section is important because by knowing them, you will be able to:

- Tell whether a software uses AI, or what kind of AI it uses
- Differentiate powerful AI solutions from weaker ones
- Determine what type of AI techniques can solve your specific business or organizational problem
- Understand some of the most popular Machine Learning and Deep Learning techniques that are being used, such as: how it analyses different types of information, how it makes predictions, how it recognizes images like your face, how it communicates with your customers, or how a robot learns to behave like humans!

The chapters included are:

- **Chapter 4: Inside the AI Laboratory**
- **Chapter 5: How AI Predicts Values and Categories**
- **Chapter 6: How AI Learns & Predicts Behaviors and Scenarios**

- **Chapter 7: How AI Communicates and Learns from Mistakes**
- **Chapter 8: How AI Starts to Think Like Humans**

Learning these is important to understand clearly and know what AI can or cannot do, and to appreciate how AI is built to perform tasks.

CHAPTER 4
Inside the AI Laboratory

One of the most interesting things about artificial intelligence is that most of the basic tasks are preprogrammed in standardized codes that we can use and reuse. That does not mean that we do not need to customize the AI model, but there is a reason China introduced AI textbooks for preschoolers! (1). In this chapter, we will see what that secret place is where AI is created, and the blueprint that most algorithms follow.

Structure

In this chapter, we will discuss the following topics:

- Labeled and unlabeled data
- Supervised, unsupervised and semi-supervised learning
- AI modeling platforms
- Components of AI models
- Steps to creating AI models
- Training and testing AI models
- Overview of major AI techniques

Objective

After studying this chapter, you should be able to:

- Understand how much control you have over a given AI model's results and how much supervision it needs

- Appreciate the essential steps and elements that are involved in AI modeling by your engineers

- Understand how AI results are tested and performance is improved

- Get a sense of the major AI techniques and the problems they help solve

4.1 Data and models

Most code snippets used to build AI are standardized and only require tweaking to suit the specific problems that they are trying to solve. Almost 70 percent of the time is usually spent preparing and pre-processing the data to be analyzed by the model rather than in writing the code itself (2). The data can be labeled so that it identifies what each piece of information in the dataset represents. For example, in the following figure, the label **TEMPERATURE** at the top of the first column indicates what the numbers in this column are:

TEMPERATURE	TIME OF ARRIVAL	DAY	COMMUTE	TEA AVAILABILITY
15 °C	6 PM	Monday	Walk	Yes
5 °C	9 PM	Tuesday	Walk	Yes
10 °C	6:30 PM	Friday	Walk	Yes
-10 °C	8 PM	Thursday	Car	No
0 °C	9:30 PM	Friday	Car	No
5 °C	7:30 PM	Monday	Car	Yes

Figure 4.1: Labeled data

As you can see in the headings in the next table, it can also be *unlabeled*:

15 °C	6 PM	Monday	Walk	Yes
5 °C	9 PM	Tuesday	Walk	Yes
10 °C	6:30 PM	Friday	Walk	Yes
-10 °C	8 PM	Thursday	Car	No
0 °C	9:30 PM	Friday	Car	No
8 °C	7:30 PM	Monday	Car	Yes

Figure 4.2: Unlabeled data

Likewise, machine learning models can be built to be supervised, unsupervised, semi-supervised, or reinforced. While supervised learning can give us predictions based on patterns, unsupervised learning can give us segmentations.

If we knew exactly the types of drinks that Maya has on any particular evening—water or tea—the ingredients that are used, and the recipe to prepare them, we would use **supervised learning**, where we would feed in labeled data and give specific instructions to the robot's AI model to decide which drink to serve on which day, and how to prepare it.

However, if we had no clue of the types of drinks Maya may choose to have, or what conditions influenced her choice or drank on any particular day, we may use **unsupervised learning** to let the model figure out patterns in Maya's preference and take decisions on its own. The data that would be used in this case can be unlabeled.

Usually, we use **semi-supervised learning**, where we know what Maya will have in terms of either water or tea, but we let the model decide the specific nuances of when she might prefer one over the other. The data is labeled to a small extent, with the rest remaining unlabeled. AI can give us richer insights with unsupervised methods, but we would have to trust it blindly. That might be okay in certain cases, such as recognizing the image of a person, where we don't necessarily need an explanation on how the AI arrived at its conclusion. However, a manager would need to explain why they made a certain business decision and would, therefore, need context to ensure that they are making informed choices rather than blindly following AI. it would require AI to be supervised, which may limit the depth of analysis. A semi-supervised approach balances the two extremes, which can be useful in certain use cases.

Finally, **reinforcement learning** is extremely important as it implies teaching the robot to learn through constant feedback or reward for the right step. That, of course, brings its own set of risks and ethical dilemmas. We will see this in detail in its dedicated chapter.

4.2 AI Modeling

Where are AI models created? Coders use particular languages to write codes on a platform of choice, the way you'd write in English or French on a blackboard or a paper. Two of the popular coding languages are Python and R. These languages are written on a platform like Anaconda. Python is better for more advanced analysis like deep learning, while R is better for neat visualizations and simpler machine learning techniques. Both have amazing libraries and packages to do things efficiently.

What do we mean by 'library'? A data scientist friend of mine gave me the perfect analogy to explain this term in the context of AI. Think about the Matrix series of movies. Do you remember when Neo was learning Kung-Fu or when Trinity had to learn to fly a helicopter? The operator just uploaded libraries 'Kung-Fu' and 'helicopter' to the Matrix environment, respectively.

The **library** is a term used to describe tools that are pre-equipped to do a job. All we have to do is provide some inputs to get an output. For example, Numpy is a library that knows all mathematical calculations. Matplotlib knows how to plot numbers and graphs. And Pandas is used to import and manage data sets. Remember, AI codes are not born with the knowledge of even basic things like mathematics. Teaching them is like teaching a kid everything from scratch. Libraries help automate a lot of that. So, to perform mathematical calculations, all we have to do is import the Numpy library. Our robot then does not need to learn how to count the hours to determine how long Maya has been at work.

How are AI models created? There are three parts to it:

1. Pre-processing the data that AI will analyze
2. Writing the actual code
3. Training and testing the model for efficiency

To recap from previous chapters, any dataset has to be prepared and pre-processed to make it ready and usable for AI codes. After all, data can be incomplete. For example, the data we feed Maya's robot may have information missing on what Maya drank on some of the days last year. Data can also be of different types. For example, Maya's age over the years would be a numerical value, but her mood may be categorized as happy, neutral, or sad. The weather, on the other hand, would be numerical, too, but in a different unit. Data can also be biased. If, say, Maya was working last year but is now pursuing her doctoral studies and living a student lifestyle, her drinking patterns may change. In such a case, information about her drinking last year would be biased to a working lifestyle and not applicable to her current situation. Data scientists and engineers take all this information to clean up the data to ensure that the algorithm provides as accurate a result as possible. Inaccuracy is one of the main reasons for AI's slow adoption.

Once the data is pre-processed, we write codes depending on which AI technique or techniques we are planning to use and then modify it to suit our specific business problems.

Finally, to determine whether the AI model works, most engineers follow the 80-20 rule, particularly in the case of supervised learning. They first train the machine on 80% of historical data and then test it on the remaining 20%. For example, let's say we have the data on which beverage Maya drank over the last 50 workweeks. Her robot would look at all the inputs (that is, the time she came home, the weather outside, the day, and so on) and the corresponding outputs (that is, what she drank) in 40 of the 50 workweeks. That's 80%. It would then study these to analyze what's going on and find patterns. It would look at only the inputs in the remaining 20% of the cases, that is, the remaining ten weeks—and try to predict what Maya drank in those ten weeks. Those guesses will then be compared with what Maya drank in those ten weeks to see how accurate the robot was:

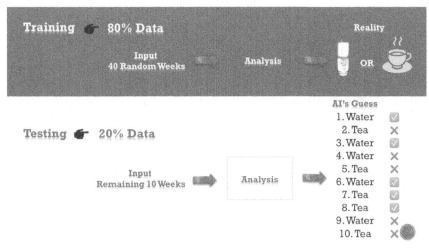

Figure 4.3: Testing the initial model

If the accuracy is low, the AI model (both the code and the input data) will be adjusted further until the accuracy improves:

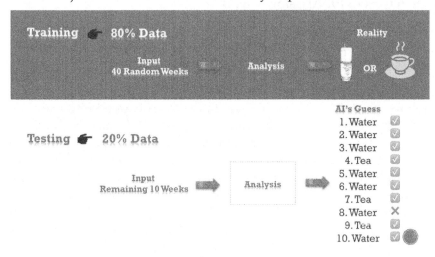

Figure 4.4: Testing the retrained model

It is why being able to see how a machine learning software determines an output is important for any AI user so that we can check the biases or inherent errors that may be in play. If we can't understand why a machine decides what it decides, how would we know whether to trust its decision? After all, the robot can learn to warm a glass of cold water by simply leaving it standing at room temperature, which will take quite a while. Instead, we can teach it to heat the water on the stove to bring it to room temperature even quicker. The effectiveness of AI naturally increases with how well trained it is, how good the data is, and how rigorous the codes are.

Having acclimatized to the AI laboratory, let us now look at all the different techniques the robot will have to apply to serve Maya her drink successfully.

4.3 Techniques overview

There are many AI solutions out there today, but how many genuinely work? How many are even genuinely AI? As we saw in Section 1, and as we will see in this section, artificial intelligence can be very simple automation of mathematical or statistical computation. It can also be something very complex and truly intelligent. A 2019 report based on a survey by London venture capital firm MMC claimed that 40% of European start-ups classified as AI companies didn't use AI in a way that was *material* to their businesses. (3). The AI label helps companies capitalize on the AI buzz, which often leads to the overuse of this term by their communications department or PR.

By the end of this section, you will have understood how to sense strong AI solutions from weaker ones. In this section, we will take Maya's robot as our guinea pig once again, and learn all the things it could ideally do to serve Maya the right beverage. There are many more AI techniques out there, but we will cover some of the most prominent ones in the next few chapters. These will include:

- **How AI predicts numbers or categories:** We will look at classification and regression techniques, as well as more advanced decision trees and ensemble learning methods to see how the robot can predict whether Maya would like water or tea.

- **How AI understands and predicts behaviors and scenarios:** Clustering will show us how the robot figures out the different types of beverage there are to choose from in the first place. Association rule learning will then allow it to figure out connections between clusters and Maya's behavior to see if she would like to have something else with her drink. Search algorithms will then explain how the robot can choose the best option with the lowest cost. We will also share a brief word on Monte Carlo Simulation, which is normally used for Risk Analysis.

- **How AI communicates and improvises:** Reinforcement Learning will show us how the robot can learn from its mistakes on the go. That includes the robot learning to walk up to Maya. With Natural Language Processing, we will then see how it can start to communicate and understand Maya when she says something to him.

- **How AI starts to think like humans:** Finally, we will go deeper into Deep Learning to understand how it can see and recognize Maya to serve her what she wants:

GOAL: SERVE MAYA HER DRINK

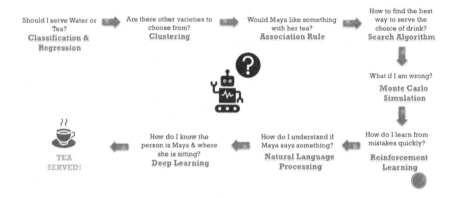

Figure 4.5: Overview of AI techniques

A thorough human-like behavior would require AI to utilize multiple techniques, as shown here. However, in practical business problem-solving, one or two of these techniques are often likely to prove sufficient. The objective here is to help you understand some of the major techniques of AI that you will come across in the context of a common example (that is, Maya's robot) for the sake of simplicity. As we go through these steps, think about the kind of problems you may be facing at work and try to break them down to understand how the different use cases could be solved using one or even a combination of these techniques.

Conclusion

As we learn about AI, it is important to appreciate the efforts that data scientists and engineers put into creating even a simple AI model. Teaching AI to do something is like teaching a child. And while libraries can help, they can only go so far. This realization is crucial also because we generally assume AI to be a smart entity capable of managing multiple facets of a task the way our human brains have become accustomed to. AI, however, is most narrow in its functionality, where it best solves a very specific set of tasks that it was designed to do.

AI can achieve outputs on its own in an unsupervised manner, by following strict and controlled guidelines in a supervised manner, or through some mix of the two. However, the fundamental steps data scientists use to create an AI model remain the same: prepare the data to be used, leverage libraries that are preprogrammed to enable certain tasks, code the rest to train the model on ~80% of the data, and test its performance on the remaining 20% of the data. In pre-processing the data, data scientists generally check if the data is properly labeled, does not have missing data, and is scaled not to get biased towards fields with larger numbers. To compare word-based information with numerical information, the data is also encoded.

The chapters that follow will help us better appreciate the work and thinking that goes into making AI capable of doing particular things, and how they all come together to achieve an objective that we humans could process much more naturally.

Questions

1. Which of the following statements are true about the unsupervised machine learning solution?

    I. The unsupervised solution does not require data to be labeled and can potentially lead to richer insights

    II. The unsupervised solution cannot explain how it arrived at a solution, thereby requiring us to follow its suggestion in an uninformed manner

    III. Unsupervised learning is generally not advisable for solutions that are critical to the business, safety, ethics, and so on, and require informed decision making

A. I & II

B. II Only

C. I, II & III

D. II & III

2. Put the basic components of creating an AI model in the right order:

I. Writing the actual code to train the model

II. Preparing the data

III. Testing the model on the part of the dataset

IV. Importing the right libraries

V. Tweaking the code to improve accuracy

A. I > II > III > IV > V

B. V > IV > III > II > I

C. IV > II > I > III > V

D. II > IV > I > III > V

3. My engineers decided to train the machine learning model on 50% of the dataset, and test it on the remaining 50%. Compared to the usual policy of training on 80% data and testing on 20%, this new approach would:

I. Ensure more rigorous testing of whether the model works

II. Lead to lesser accuracy of insights if 50% of the data is not enough in volume to train the model on

A. I Only

B. II Only

C. Both I & II

D. Neither I nor II

4. Is this statement true or false? Artificial Intelligence capabilities in software do not mean that it will always be better than software that runs mathematical or statistical computation without AI, in solving a business problem.

5. Is this statement true or false? If you came across a library built to recognize images, you could simply feed images into it and get results, without the need for other steps involved in the AI modeling.

Answers

1. C

    Explanation: Unsupervised learning also does not require labeled data. It can also be risky if critical decisions have to be made by managers without clearly understanding how the AI solution arrived at its insights, in case there are errors in the analysis.

2. C

    Explanation: A common practice is to import the required libraries upfront for easy reference and also because some, like pandas, may be used in Data Pre-processing itself. All work on the code follows next.

3. C

    Explanation: 50% of the data, assuming sufficient overall volume for AI, are a lot of cases to test AI's accuracy on, which ensures rigor. However, it can also mean fewer data available for the AI model to be trained on in the first place. That is particularly true if the remaining 50% of the data does not constitute enough volume and diversity to represent all the different scenarios that the AI model has to learn.

4. True

    Explanation: Even the simplest AI with basic automation of computations can be useful in practice and offer greater convenience and speed. However, that does not guarantee that it would be more robust in solving a use case than a non-AI software. The latter may utilize significantly greater, more diverse, and more relevant computations for a given use case, even if they are not automated.

5. False

    Explanation: Some level of data pre-processing, coding, training, and testing is always needed for an AI model to perform well.

CHAPTER 5
How AI Predicts Values and Categories

The most common way that machine learning is used to make predictions is using classification, and regression techniques, together often referred to as CART. The difference is in the type of predictions they make. Regression techniques help predict constant value, such as numbers. So, we would use it to answer a question like when is Maya likely to return today—6:00 p.m., 6:30 p.m., 7 p.m., and so on? Classification helps predict a non-continuous value such as category or type. The question it would answer would, therefore, be: what type of drink will Maya like to drink if she returns at 6 p.m. today—water or tea? Note that we are talking about supervised learning here. Let's look at how this works.

Structure

In this chapter, we will discuss the following topics:

- Introduction to classification
    - o K-nearest neighbor method
    - o Support vector machine
    - o The business value of classification

- Introduction to regression
  - o Linear and non-linear regression
  - o The business value of regression
- Decision trees and Ensemble learning
  - o Decision trees
  - o Ensemble learning
  - o The business value of decision trees and ensemble methods

Objective

After studying this chapter, you should be able to:

- Understand how an AI solution that uses classification works
- Understand how an AI solution that uses regression works
- Decide which types of problems can be best solved by classification and which ones by regression
- Tell when a CART-based AI solution is strong or weak
- Understand how Machine Learning makes CART powerful
- Watch out for errors in the results you get from CART
- Learn the real-world applications of these techniques

5.1 Classification

Classification is applied in many fields, from medicine to marketing. In almost all classification techniques, all known categorical data, that is, data having categories—is plotted on a graph. When a new piece of data emerges, the machine learning model decides which of the existing categories that particular information belongs to. It then assigns that data to the corresponding category. To understand this, think about the news you may have come across on how AI can help predict storms and cyclones. The approach behind this machine learning solution is simply to look for the rotational movement in clouds or the category of 'comma-shaped clouds'—which helps it predict 64% of severe weather events. (1). How it sees and recognizes those comma-shaped clouds, is something we will cover in Deep Learning when we learn image recognition.

Let's look at two classification methods that will help us understand this technique better.

5.1.1 K-nearest neighbor

One is called the K nearest neighbor or KNN method. In this method, when new data emerges, the model picks the 'K' nearest values to that point on the graph. So, if K = 3, the model will pick the three nearest values to a data point. The category that the majority of those chosen values belong to is likely the one that the new value belongs to as well. For example, let's say Maya's robot plots the drinks she has had in the last year - water or tea - on a graph. The x-axis denotes the temperature outside from -15 degrees Celsius to +15 degrees Celsius, and the y-axis denotes the time of arrival from 5 p.m. to 9 p.m. The next time when Maya comes home from the office, the robot plots her time of arrival and temperature outside on this graph, picks the three nearest values, and checks which category they belong to:

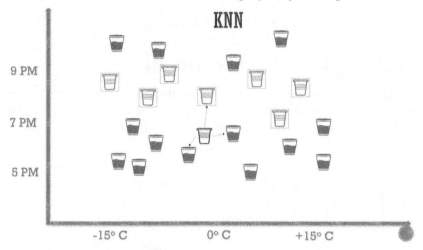

Figure 5.1: KNN in action - I

Once the new data point is categorized as per the category of the majority of those nearest three data points, the robot knows what to serve Maya.

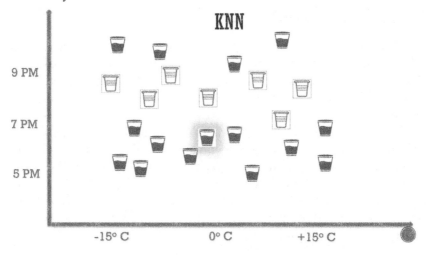

Figure 5.2: KNN in action - II

5.1.2 Support vector machine

Another classification method is called SVM or support vector machine. In this technique, the robot finds the outside temperature and time combination for water that is closest to tea on the graph:

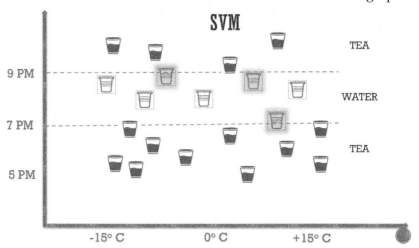

Figure 5.3: SVM in Action - I

It then finds the combination of tea that is closest to water:

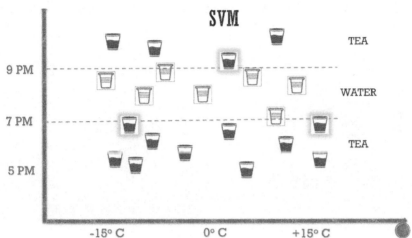

Figure 5.4: SVN in Action - II

The robot is effectively trying to plot the boundaries of weather and time combinations when Maya may want tea or water. Upon her next arrival, it would simply look at the weather-time combination and check which of these two points, it is closest to and determines whether Maya would like tea or water.

We learned earlier that there are two types of values we generally deal with: Continuous like numbers, which regression helps with, or Non-continuous like categories, which classification helps with. Data, however, can also be linear, which means it can be divided by a simple line on a graph. Or it can be non-linear, which means it cannot.

The choice of the KNN or SVM method depends on the kind of data set that is being used because of the difference in the two approaches. KNN may be better if you have a lot of data points but on a lower dimension scale. SVM is generally better when higher dimensions are involved. What does that mean? Consider the following graph:

2D   3D

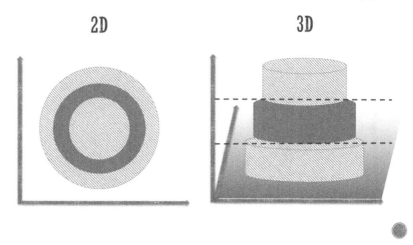

Figure 5.5: Converting a 2D model into 3D

Let's say the first graph, which is 2-dimensional, looks at only the temperature and time variables. A simple line cannot divide the two types of data (shaded light and dark respectively) in the image on the left as it is a 2D graph with circles. However, if we consider a third dimension—the day of the week, we can convert this 2D graph into a 3D, and the task becomes much easier, as shown in the image on the right. On a related note, Facebook has developed AI that can convert 2D objects into 3D shapes. It detects and classifies the various objects in an image, and predicts the corresponding three-dimensional shapes. (2).

Depending on the answer you're looking for a continuous number on a non-continuous category, you may choose regression or classification. But then again, depending on the kind of data you have at hand for the machine learning solution, you may choose KNN classification or SVM classification. And that is how you approach deciding the kind of techniques you want to go to address a given business problem.

5.1.3 The business value of Classification

KNN is commonly used in organizations due to its ease of use and lack of any prior assumption on the data. For instance, mapping the movie preference of a group of customers and their profiles can allow Netflix to determine which movie a similar customer is likely to prefer based on his/her profile. This use case is also where Association Rules come in handy, which we will discuss in the next chapter.

KNN can similarly help companies classify the ideal salary levels of individuals based on their office locations around the world or their skill, in comparison to the prevalent best practice in that region in the industry. A similar logic can also reveal pay discrepancies by gender or race. KNN also helps reveal potential credit card frauds based on the usage pattern. More importantly, it can classify a new customer as a potential fraud or a high-spending VIP based on patterns related to his/her profile in comparison to other customers with similar profiles.

In short, for a business, any use case where an entity or situation has to be classified based on similar other entities or situations is where KNN can be a quick and effective method.

The multi-dimensional classification capability of SVM can prove handy in any image-based analysis. In a way, the image here can refer to anything we see. We briefly discussed earlier in the chapter, the value of classification in detecting cyclonic cloud formation using image recognition. The specific technique applied is often SVM. And that approach also helps our phone cameras or Facebook automatically detect faces in a picture. We will learn how AI recognizes images in the chapter on Deep Learning. However, once an image is recognized, the different features in an image can be classified using SVM, for example, faces versus non-faces.

An AI model can use the same approach to automatically understand the hand-written text on a paper by classifying varying images of each letter into its respective digital character. So, images of the letter 'A' hand-written in any style can all be classified as A. SVM can also help analyze the text by its size to classify them as headings and non-headings. The headings can then be further analyzed to classify the document or article in a particular category, say, business or sports. Text analysis uses Natural Language Processing, which we will see later as well.

The SVM approach can be useful for the finance team dealing with hard-copies of invoices or bills that can be auto-read to populate information on a system. In research labs, SVM can similarly be used to classify digital images of microbes or molecules into specific classes or types.

All these examples deal with categorical data, but these use cases can be further bolstered if we could also predict continuous values. It's time now to look at how machine learning achieves that with regression.

5.2 Regression

In the previous example, Maya's robot decided what she's likely to drink based on when she comes home and the weather outside. To be efficient, our dear robot now wants to have Maya's drink ready by the time she comes home. However, while it knows the expected weather in the evening, it doesn't know when Maya will likely come home today. So, it decides to predict her time of arrival. The technique it therefore uses is called **regression**.

The concept of regression is similar to classification: It maps out all known information on a graph to try and see if there are patterns that may help predict unknown information. But how does it work? Imagine if Maya's robot looked at the day of the week and the time that Maya has come home each day so far and plotted it on a graph. Through regression, the robot can now check if there is consistency in Maya's behavior that can, therefore, help it predict when she is likely to come home, given a specific day of the week:

Figure 5.6: *Linear regression in action*

Before we proceed, let's spare a thought to this: In day to day life, we do not have a record of our time of arrival for each day last year. So, Maya's robot will have to wait while it records the arrival time each day that Maya comes home until it starts to see a pattern. That may take a few weeks, a few months or even a year. So, companies are not always ready to use AI or get results from AI instantly, particularly if it requires internal data that the company has to provide but doesn't have at hand. It is also why organizations that plan to lead in AI must start getting their data ready and get a data dictionary in place first.

What we saw in our graph is a case of a simple linear regression that looks at just one factor: the day of the week influencing Maya's time of arrival. What if it was dependent on more than one condition such as those Friday night parties that Maya tends to have. That would be a case of multiple linear regression:

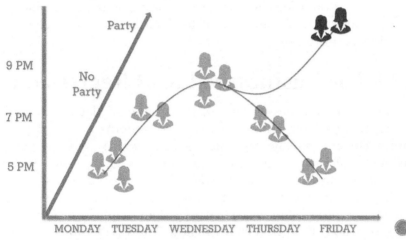

Figure 5.7: Multiple linear regression in action

Just as in classification, there can also be situations where the correlation is not so straightforward. We can then use **SVR** or **Support Vector Regression**, in both linear and nonlinear conditions, that may also involve plotting the graph on a higher dimension as we saw earlier.

We should be careful when using Regression, particularly when two independent variables may be closely correlated to each other - an issue called **Multicollinearity**. Let's say Maya's robot tried to look at not only the weather outside but also Maya's commute, to see if her choice to drive or walk influences the drink she has once home. It may find that Maya mostly has hot stuff when she drives back home but has cold stuff when she walks back. But wait. It could be a false pattern. It could be that Maya mostly takes her car to work in winter months when the temperature is always below freezing. And she chooses to walk in summer months when it's much warmer outside. In this case, the weather itself is influencing the type of commute and is also likely influencing the temperature of the drink. The robot's assessment would, therefore, be wrong because if Maya takes a car on a summer day, she may still prefer something cold rather than hot!

Another issue is **Endogeneity**, where not only do changes in one variable influence changes in another, just the way weather influences commute, but also vice versa. Such nuances can make building a robust regression model often much more demanding than other machine learning techniques. These errors are also classic examples of why the human interpretation of a prediction is so important. It is why you should look for, as far as feasible, and explainable AI solution where you can understand the logic behind AI's prediction to decide if it makes sense.

5.2.1 The business value of Regression

Similar to how businesses can use patterns in similar information to classify new information, they can use patterns in past data to extrapolate and estimate continuous values, which can even be the probability of categorical values. To explain the latter, consider an insurance company that uses KNN to classify a car owner's profile as a high-risk for accidents. It can now plugin Regression models to estimate the probability of the accident claim within a certain time frame or value. That, in turn, can allow it to decide on premiums based on the risk profile and an estimate of what and when the cost will likely be incurred. Regression can also help the company estimate the collective cost burden across the entire population of different risk profiles.

Another example would be the ability to predict sales in the next quarter by looking at the sales in the last few quarters or the same quarter in the last few years (for seasonal businesses). The same logic can help a company estimate the **return on investment (ROI)** over a certain period on its spend on a marketing initiative—either as per the results trend so far or as per the results trend historically with similar investments in the past. Such use cases allow companies to forecast revenue (or costs) and plan the budget accordingly.

Regression can also help predict the footfall or demand for a particular item in a retail store. For example, Walmart installed the **Intelligent Retail Lab (IRL),** in one of its stores to manage the inventory levels based on the expected demand. They have cameras installed in the store to detect products on the shelf (Image Recognition) constantly, distinguish them accurately (for example, a small packet of Lays versus a family pack) and alert the staff on which products may need to be re-stocked on the shelf based on the expected demand on the day. (3).

As a handy mental note, any use case where you would like to predict a future *number* based on past or incoming data may be a good place to use regression.

The techniques we have looked at so far are useful for linear problems, but they are not the most advanced when it comes to nonlinear problems. If you're looking for a machine learning software that uses CART or solves these kinds of problems, you should check whether it uses even stronger techniques such as decision trees and ensemble learning. Let's look at how these make Machine Learning solutions even more powerful.

5.3 Decision Trees and Ensemble Learning

We discussed earlier how a machine learning solution could be something quite simple or complex, something weak or really powerful. We will now see just how the CART prediction techniques become even more powerful due to the depth and rigor of their analysis in machine learning through techniques like decision trees and enhanced ensemble learning methods like bagging and boosting.

5.3.1 Decision Trees

Decision trees first. It works as follows: Imagine a graph plotting Maya's time of arrival and the weather outside. We take a variable, say, the time of Maya's arrival and choose a point to split it into two conditions. Let's say this point is 7 p.m. The resultant conditions are Maya arriving before 7 p.m, and after 7 p.m. We then split one of these conditions on the second variable, say, the weather outside. For example, when Maya arrives after 7 p.m., the robot should check whether the temperature outside is more than 0°C or less. It is followed by a further sub condition—the third split. For example, if Maya arrives after 7 p.m. and the temperature is less than 0°C, check whether Maya arrived before or after 9 p.m. Consequently, if Maya has arrived after 7 p.m., it is colder than 0°C and Maya have arrived before 9 p.m., the robot should serve her hot tea:

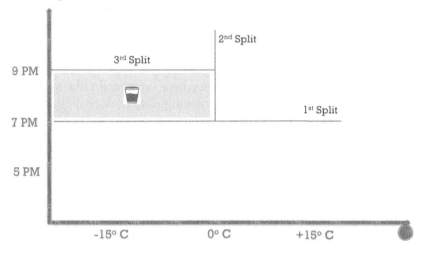

Figure 5.8: Decision tree model in action

Decision trees are very useful when there are multiple independent variables. As you can see, a decision tree can have many branches, with each branch corresponding to a new decision. A good ML model determines just how many splits to make, that is, how many branches this tree should have. Both too many or too few are not a good thing. The split points are generally decided in such a way that each split divides the different choices. It is the learning process of the machine learning model.

5.3.2 Ensemble Learning

A more powerful decision tree technique is called random forest. As the name suggests, a forest consists of many *trees*. In other words, random forest involves a lot of decision trees created for each data point.

It is also called **ensemble learning**, where you either take multiple decision tree algorithms or the same decision tree algorithm multiple times and use it to create something more powerful. Decision trees are helpful when you want to interpret results, understand what's going on, and determine how the results are being calculated. But if you're just looking for high performance, the random forest would be better. Ensemble methods like random forest are powerful because they help avoid irrelevant or biased data in the analysis. How is that? Due to the use of many models, the errors get middle out. It is one of the fundamental concepts of AI. Just the way it assumes that there are patterns in any given situation, it also assumes that the more we progressively analyze or study something, the lower the errors become even if they don't reach zero.

Ensemble learning makes machine learning even more powerful by working in two ways: Bagging and Boosting. Random forest is a bagging technique where we build many independent models or decision trees and combine, or *bag* them. Boosting, on the other hand, is when we build models sequentially, each getting boosted by learning from the errors of the previous ones. In other words, each Decision tree learns from the mistake of the previous decision trees to become more powerful. Note that ensemble learning techniques can be similarly applied to other models as well:

ENSEMBLE LEARNING

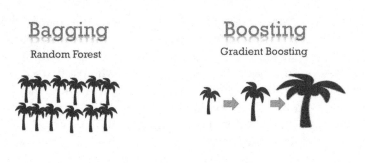

Bagging
Random Forest

Boosting
Gradient Boosting

Figure 5.9: Bagging versus Boosting

An example of such a powerful technique is called Gradient Boosting. Its approach is simple. Let's say we started with a simple AI model, a simple tree in this case, which naturally has low accuracy and contains errors. We analyze those specific data points that seem to be a misfit and leading to errors, as well as how the values have been classified or arranged. When we revise the AI model next, we will focus specifically on those problematic data points and try to get them right. The process continues as the model evolves, each version resulting in lower errors and better accuracy. That does not, once again, mean that the longer we evolve the model, the better the results would be. As mentioned before, there is always a sweet spot—a point which yields more or less the best result that we should stop at.

Decision trees have several benefits over a simple linear regression. It works much better with data that is a mix of numeric, such as Maya's arrival time, and unconditional, such as Maya's drink. Decision trees also handle missing information more gracefully, whereas, for other methods, we will have to fill in the missing data in the dataset by estimating that at the time of data pre-processing before we get into coding. For classification, decision trees can also draw more complex borders between different categories. If you recall KNN or SVM, the categorization was dependent on a clear spread of the different points. Decision trees would be able to define the boundaries at which water or tea exists more crisply.

5.3.3 The business value of Decision Trees and Ensemble Learning

The value of ensemble learning can be attributed to nearly every use case where we would apply a classification or regression technique, as discussed earlier. It can allow us to leverage predicting numbers or classes on another level. For example, Microsoft used Random Forest for its Kinect gaming platform, where they mapped our movements in the air to quickly and accurately predict 3D positions of body joints. (4). Random Forest can also allow a robust analysis of various product features (say, the product packaging or content for B2C companies) to gauge consumer interest based on past success. It can even analyze the various aspects of machinery and its usage conditions to predict its longevity, or features of a food item to estimate its expiry or quality.

Gradient boosting can also be useful in such cases and, in fact, even lend higher accuracy at times. For instance, it could help predict the likelihood of a customer's retention by analyzing many more factors than her profile, product purchase, or timing. These could include her monthly purchases, customer support volumes, upsells, and so on. The idea is to be able to leverage a significantly greater number of variables for accurate results than would otherwise be possible with the individual model (or trees), which each of these cases of bagging or boosting utilizes.

Decision trees themselves can prove very useful in helping make decisions. Thanks to them, Gerber was able to decide whether to continue using PVC plastic in its baby products. Once PVC was claimed to be dangerous by Greenpeace ahead of an upcoming peak Christmas season, Gerber quickly used Decision trees to weigh in the consequences of two equally risky options—to wait for consumer response to PVC-based toys or to remove that key ingredient from their product proactively. Analyzing the cost and revenue impact based on estimates in the series of decisions, involved in either case, allowed it to make a prudent choice. (5).

Decision trees can similarly help businesses make a lot of other decisions—from deciding which venture to invest in, to operational allocations in manufacturing factories. It can also help analyze portfolio gains in the scenario of different interest rates, manage inventory levels based on demand fluctuations, or help decide which complementary products to launch from a set of options that a company can afford. In short, decision trees can be considered where trade-offs or predictions in different scenarios have to be made.

In this chapter, we have seen how the robot decides when Maya would arrive and which drink she would like. But how did it figure out how many different types of drinks there are to choose from in the first place? In our next lesson, we will use clustering to answer this. It will allow us to see just then how AI starts to work around more complicated analysis, like behavior tracking and risk management, which allows marketers to understand the similar or different types of customers you and I may be, understand our behaviors, and manage the risk of being wrong.

Conclusion

Classification and regression techniques are two of the essential techniques you are likely to find in software, particularly when it is tasked with predicting categories (non-continuous values) or numbers (continuous values), respectively. There are various ways of executing classification or regression, and each technique has its pros and cons related to how good the result looks, how much flexibility we have in seeing data in different dimensions or how the data is spread out. However, we must always watch out for errors like Multicollinearity or Endogeneity that can often lead us to incorrect conclusions from an AI software employing either of these techniques.

CART is further bolstered in machine learning with decision trees and ensemble learning techniques. Decision trees allow applying CART when multiple independent variables are involved, which cannot be easily processed by conventional methods. Given that AI's strength lies in finding hidden patterns by taking into account variables, we may not otherwise consider, decision trees serve as a classic example of this ability in action. Ensemble learning strengthens these trees/models further by employing one of two approaches: Bagging multiple models together or boosting each iteratively into a stronger one. Random forest and gradient boosting are examples of each, respectively.

Questions

1. In which of the following cases would I likely use classification techniques, and in which would I likely use regression techniques:

    I. Predict the duration for which a machine can operate at peak performance in summer versus winter months

    II. Find the probability of a sales deal closing in the next quarter

    III. Based on the above probability, predict whether the sales deal will be won or lost

    IV. Determine which of the potential feature additions to our product will likely appeal to our Millennial audience segment

    A. II & III will require Classification. I & IV will require Regression.

    B. II, III & IV will require Classification. I will require Regression.

    C. III & IV will require Classification. I & II will require Regression.

    D. All will require Classification.

2. Which of the following approach does random forest follow, and is it bagging or boosting technique:

    I. Build many independent models and combine them

    II. Build models sequentially, each improving on the errors of the previous model to become better

    A. I only, and it is a Bagging technique

    B. I only, and it is a Boosting technique

    C. II only, and it is a Bagging technique

    D. II only, and it is a Boosting technique

3. Which of the following is always true for why decision trees are better than linear regression:

    I.   They can handle missing data better

    II. They also work well with data that is a mix of numeric and categorical

    III. They can explain the underlying logic behind their solution

    A. All of them

    B. II & III

    C. I Only

    D. I & II

4. Is this statement true or false? Gradient boosting works because it iteratively builds a stronger model by addressing the errors in the previous model.

5. When higher dimensions are involved in classification, it is generally better to use the .... technique.

Answers

1. C

    Explanation: I & II require predicting or identifying numeric or continuous values, and will require Regression. III & IV require predicting or identifying categorical values and will use Classification. Note that we can do binary Classification (for example, win/lose prediction) with a Regression algorithm (for example, "win" if the prediction is above 50%, "lose" if the prediction is below 50%).

2. A
3. D
4. True
5. SVM

CHAPTER 6

How AI Learns and Predicts Behaviors and Scenarios

Numbers and categories are relatively tangible entities, predicting which can be achieved statistically to varying degrees of accuracy. But how do we tackle something more intangible and subjective? These are situations where unsupervised learning starts to become more helpful, especially when we do not know the situational abstracts well enough to supervise the AI on set parameters. A good example would be predicting human behavior or the risk involved in a given situation. Even to classify objects, we must first decide what categories exist in a given population. How does AI achieve all that?

Structure

In this chapter, we will discuss the following topics:

- Introduction to clustering
  - o K-means clustering
  - o Hierarchical clustering
  - o The business value of clustering

- Introduction association rules
  - o Apriori and Eclat methods
  - o The business value of association rules
- Search algorithms and Monte Carlo Simulation
  - o Search algorithms – Uninformed and Informed
  - o The business value of search algorithms

Objective

After studying this chapter, you should be able to:

- Identify the distinct groups of entities that exist in a population
- Find correlations between different behaviors among people in a certain group
- Understand how AI minimizes the risk of being wrong
- Determine how AI searches and finds any information
- Learn the real-world applications of these techniques

6.1 Clustering

Clustering is similar to classification in that it also deals with categories. Only, we don't know what categories exist in a population from the start. For Maya's robot, there can be many types of drinks in existence potentially—water, tea, coffee, soda, juice, and so on. Clustering can help it identify the different types of drinks that exist in Maya's home or are in her consideration each day. It often reveals categories that we would not even have realized otherwise.

A common example would be marketers trying to identify the different types of customers that buy the company's products, HR's trying to segment the different types of employees to gauge their motivation and performance levels, or traders are trying to cluster the different stock types to gauge expected returns. How is it done? There are several methods. We look at two over here: K means clustering and hierarchical clustering.

6.1.1 K-means Clustering

In the K-means method, let's say Maya's robot looks at the drinks she has had over the last year between 5 p.m. and midnight on a

Wednesday at home. It doesn't yet know how to differentiate these. So, we plot them all on a graph by the temperature outside and the time of consumption. Let's say it now randomly picks two points on the graph. These are called centroids:

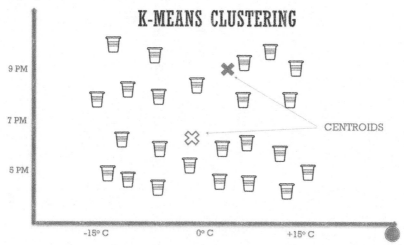

Figure 6.1: *K-means clustering in action - I*

It assigns each of the other points to its closest centroid. Now we have two clusters—the red one and the brown one:

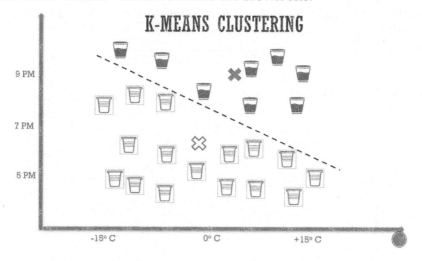

Figure 6.2: *K-means clustering in action - II*

For each cluster, the robot now finds the new centroid, which is the middle point of that cluster:

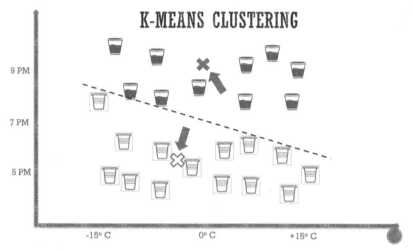

Figure 6.3: K-means clustering in action - III

It reassigns all the other points to the new centroid that they are closest to. It gives us two new clusters of red and brown. The robot once again finds the middle point of these two new clusters and repeats the process. It continues until we can no longer move the centroids, thereby giving us the final two clusters in the dataset. It is another example of AI learning by iterations:

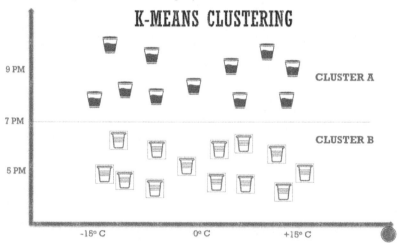

Figure 6.4: K-means clustering in Action - IV

Just like in statistics, clustering is often dependent on human interpretation. Once the machine has identified the clusters, we have to identify what differentiates them and what is common in the different objects within a cluster. In the case of the robot's clustering, it notices that cluster A and cluster B are differentiated by the color of their drink. That's great. However, we have to come in then and label these as *Tea* and *Water*, respectively, based on the primary attribute of differentiation here: say, the color of the drink.

Clustering leads us to group things by features that may not be obvious otherwise. It is more powerful because instead of segmenting people traditionally, let's say by demographics, we can profile them by hidden characteristics—their behavior, their preferences, and so on. K-means algorithms also prove very useful in online document classification based on tags, topics, or content; in identifying crime localities based on the area and type of crime; insurance fraud detection; and even helping you draft your fantasy team in sports by clustering players based on their stats! (1).

In our example, the robot has managed to cluster and differentiate water and tea by its color. But it could just as easily have chosen two different starting points and therefore ended up differentiating the drinks by their temperature:

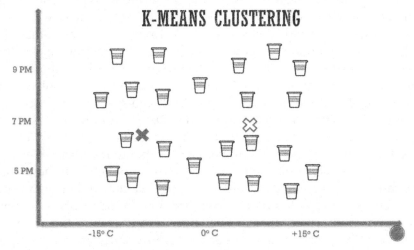

Figure 6.5: K-means clustering in action – V

In that case, we could have ended up with cluster **A** reflecting cold water and iced tea, and cluster **B** is reflecting warm water and hot tea, as shown below:

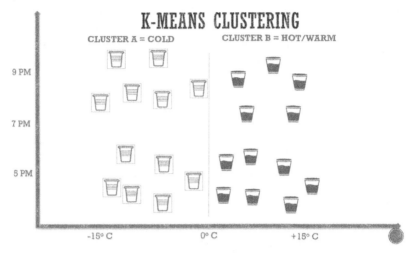

Figure 6.6: K-means clustering in action - VI

It is one of the traps of this type of clustering, where the choice of initial centroids can also lead to wrong or irrelevant clusters. You may also have noticed that K-means clustering requires us to know already how many types of drinks there are. That's why we chose two starting centroids instead of 3 or 4. To find the ideal number of clusters in a population mathematically, we use something called the **Within Cluster Sum of Squares technique (WCSS)** or the Elbow method. Without going into the mathematical formula, it looks at the distance of each point on a graph with its centroid and decreases in value with an increase in the number of clusters chosen. The resulting graph gives us the optimal number of clusters to choose from. In the figure below, the optimal number is 3, the point at which we get an elbow. Fewer clusters result in too big a distance between the points within a cluster and its centroid, implying that many points may only loosely be represented by that centroid. On the other hand, having a higher number of clusters does not seem to reduce the distance between the points and their centroid significantly. It would imply that any further breaking up of the three clusters may be immaterial as the new clusters would be relatively similar to each other:

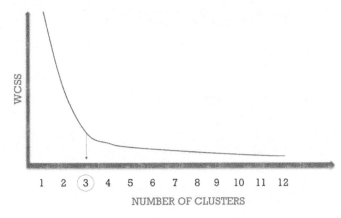

Figure 6.7: WCSS Graph

6.1.2 Hierarchical Clustering

If we do not know how many clusters or types of drinks there are, we can also use another clustering method called **hierarchical clustering**. In this method, we cluster data points step by step until we end up with one big cluster. It is called Agglomeration or Bottom-up approach. For example, let's start with one data point serving as a starting cluster:

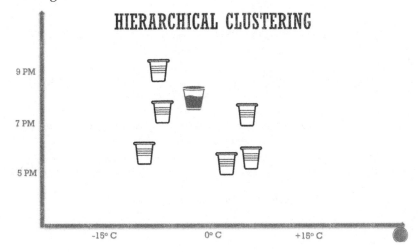

Figure 6.8: Hierarchical clustering in action – I

The next step aggregates the starting data point or *cluster* with its closest data point. Meanwhile, another data point on the farthest end that is equally or closer to a different data point can serve as another starting cluster:

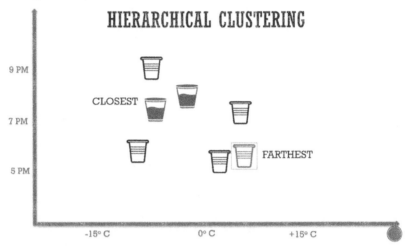

Figure 6.9: *Hierarchical clustering in action – II*

The next step follows the same aggregation logic for both starting clusters or points:

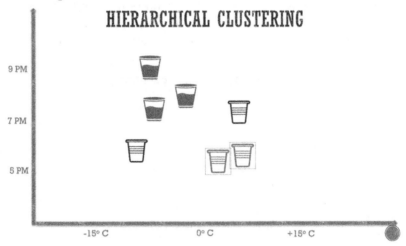

Figure 6.10: *Hierarchical clustering in action – III*

We eventually reach a point where only two clusters remain:

Figure 6.11: Hierarchical clustering in action - IV

We can also go in reverse, starting with one big cluster and declustering points one by one, which would be a divisive or top-down approach. Either way, at the end of each step, we record it on a special graph called **Dendrogram**, which helps us show the hierarchical relationship between clusters. Clustering is a traditional statistical technique, but machine learning has made it more effective because the AI model can now maintain a memory of how clusters look at the end of each step of the process. It stores that information, that memory, in a Dendrogram. The lines represent distances that are measured between clusters after each step of clustering/declustering. The distance represents the degree of dissimilarity between clusters at each step, thereby revealing the clearest number of clusters that are most distinctly apart:

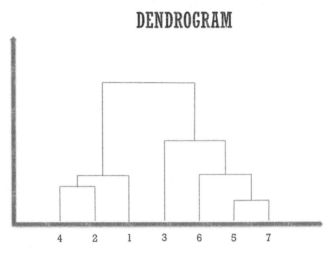

Figure 6.12: Sample Dendrogram

How do we choose between K-means and hierarchical clustering, though? K-means clustering is easy to understand, but it needs us first to choose the number of clusters. In Maya's case, this method may be suitable. But if we can't define the number of clusters, hierarchical clustering would be better. However, hierarchical clustering ironically does not work as well with large datasets.

6.1.3 The business value of Clustering

The business applications of clustering can closely follow the examples we saw in CART. For instance, just as SVM helped analyze documents to classify them in business or sports category, K-means can be used to determine the categories themselves or to group similar documents based on their content, tags, or title.

We used the Elbow method to identify the optimal number of clusters. That logic can allow a logistics company to identify the optimal clusters or areas for delivery of goods by a single truck. It can help the company assess the number of trucks needed and the time taken per truck while also saving costs on fleet management.

Cities can identify cluster areas similarly within their jurisdiction by the level of crime, population growth, or commerce-to-resident ratios to plan their police force allocation, transit levels, amenities provisions, development needs, or expected revenue—all of which can help city planning with clustering as the main tool.

Customer support teams in businesses can group the callers by type of request or concern, the timing of the calls, the area the callers belong to, or the product they have questions regarding. All these can, again, allow businesses to manage the customer support staffing and operations most cost-effectively, while also providing critical feedback on any important areas of concern among its consumers.

We had briefly mentioned the examples of Marketers and HR's earlier. Banks can use it to segment loan applicants based on their risk profiles or potential earning, for example. A recent MBA graduate is likely to have a distinct earning, spending, and saving pattern, different from a soon-to-retire executive. As a thumb rule, segmenting customers or employees on a host of parameters as per the business question at hand is often something you can consider using clustering for. The same goes for any grouping-related question. The choice of clustering in each of these use cases would depend on the difference between K-means and hierarchical techniques we discussed earlier.

That brings us to the end of clustering. Thanks to this and the exploits of the previous chapter, Maya's robot is aware of the drinks to choose from when Maya's likely to arrive, and what to serve when she does arrive. But Maya is very impressed by how Netflix knows what else she may like to watch tonight, and she wants her robot to learn that skill too. We will now look at how the robot can learn that by assessing Maya's behavior.

6.2 Association Rules

Have you ever wondered how Netflix recommends the next movie you may want to watch? One of the many techniques that it employs is association rules. Association Rule Mining helps us make predictions based on behaviors. As a result, 75% of what people watch on Netflix comes from recommendations. 35% of Amazon sales come from recommendations as well. It also helps websites like TechCrunch host chatbots that keep track of what each person reads and deliver articles they may like. Pinterest takes it a step further by not only connecting users with pins of interest but also removing spam or irrelevant ones. (2).

At its heart, Association Rule Mining can help answer a simple question such as: if a person buys milk, is he or she also likely to buy bread? Let's look at two association rule methods to understand this technique more: Apriori and Eclat.

6.2.1 Apriori

The **Apriori method** works by analyzing similar behaviors in a given population. That could mean looking at the behaviors of Maya and her colleagues in the office. However, for ease of understanding, let's consider Maya's situation in isolation. Let's say that out of 300 working days last year, when Maya had her evening beverage after coming back from work, Maya took a cookie with it on 150 days. In other words, she ate the cookie 50% of the time. It is called **Support**. Now suppose that out of those 300 working days, Maya drank tea on 200 days after work last year. Her robot finds that it was out of these 200 days that Maya ate a cookie (on 150 days). In other words, she ate a cookie 75% of the time when she had tea. It is called **Confidence**.

The Apriori method helps because if the robot had to randomly predict whether Maya would like a cookie with a drink, the chances of it being right would have been 50%. But it now knows that every time Maya has tea, there's a 75% chance she will have a cookie too. That improvement in the robot's odds of being right is called Lift. It is calculated as confidence divided by support, or in this case, 1.5:

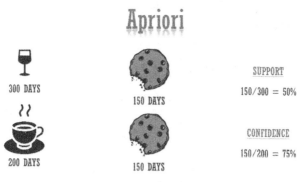

Apriori

300 DAYS

150 DAYS

SUPPORT
150/300 = 50%

200 DAYS

150 DAYS

CONFIDENCE
150/200 = 75%

LIFT = CONFIDENCE/SUPPORT = 75% / 50% = 1.5

Figure 6.13: Apriori in action

In machine learning, we normally set the minimum support and confidence that we are willing to consider. So, only behaviors that have a higher association than a certain minimum is considered. That works well if we have a large dataset, as in real-life business cases where there are a lot of instances of Maya having tea with or without a cookie. If we have a smaller dataset and want to explore more potential associations, such as tea-cookie, water-cookie, tea-bread, and so on, then we can use the Eclat method.

6.2.2 Eclat

In the Eclat method, we only look at Support; no Confidence and no Lift. We pre-decide the minimum Support that we are willing to accept, sort all associations in order of decreasing Support to identify the best ones, and cut off the ones that don't meet the threshold:

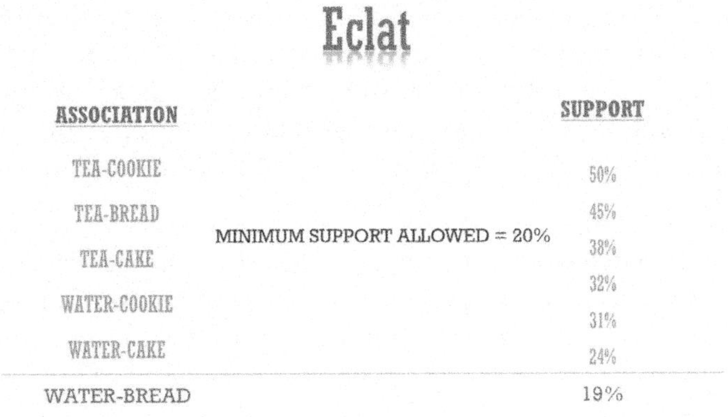

Eclat

ASSOCIATION		SUPPORT
TEA-COOKIE		50%
TEA-BREAD		45%
TEA-CAKE	MINIMUM SUPPORT ALLOWED = 20%	38%
		32%
WATER-COOKIE		31%
WATER-CAKE		24%
WATER-BREAD		19%

Figure 6.14: Eclat in action

6.2.3 The business value of Association Rules

Association rules are essentially useful every time we have to find an association, and group things by it or make predictions based on it. That makes them helpful in a broad array of scenarios. You would also be right in seeing some linkage here to clustering. The two methods—Association rules and clustering—can support each other well. Let's go back to our Netflix example to understand this more.

If Netflix identified a cluster of the audience that is mainly interested in horror movies, it would only suggest horror movies to that audience group all the time. In such a case, applying association rules could help identify if some people in this group may also like a non-horror movie since everyone likes a change once in a while. It would allow Netflix to re-segment its audience into clusters that are not genre-specific but say, mood-specific. It could then suggest a horror movie to the same viewer on the weekend or near Halloween, but a comedy movie on a tiring weekday.

I recall another example of how association rules revealed the uncanny linkage between beers and diapers. (3). These two products were very often being purchased together in a store at certain times in a day. While unbelievable at first, it was found that these specific diaper purchases were being made by fathers running errands while the mothers were taking care of the babies. And the beer was a pleasure purchase for these consumers. The store was now well-positioned to send out offers, timely reminders to fathers on other products of interest, or to simply place beers beside diapers at key times to enhance basket value from the fathers—a hidden opportunity that a store would never otherwise associate with the sale of diapers.

The above examples also show us how machine learning becomes stronger when we apply a mix of techniques, say, clustering and association rules, and how machine learning is better at understanding hidden or complex information such as our personal preferences on different dates.

Association rules could help unravel the chances of an abnormally cold winter in N. America every time the year sees an El Nino effect. It could help HR's predict patterns in employees leaving the company to reduce churn and ensure it is staffed as per its requirement. Finance teams could dig deeper to find associations to rise in costs, which is generally obvious for seasonal businesses. Economists could predict to a slightly higher degree of accuracy, fluctuations in the economy linked to certain human-made or natural events. Discernible behavior patterns could allow authorities to ensure crowd-control or event managers to ensure a successful response based on how the sounds and lighting are tuned to the audience. A shop can use a similar approach to facilitate and increase sales. To think of it, the concept of association rules can even date back millennia to astrologers who would foretell calamities based on the star-patterns in the sky!

Maya's robot has been able to accurately identify when she is likely to come home, which we saw in regression, and what to serve Maya today, which we saw in classification. We now also know the associations to serve to Maya—perhaps it's hot tea with a cookie. But the robot can never be 100% confident with any of these choices. AI always works in probabilities. So how does the robot account for risks? More importantly, at every step, the robot has to choose the best way to do something, even with opening the cookie pack. So how does it continually find the best approach to take and minimizes the risks associated with the wrong approaches? We conclude this chapter by starting to look at how AI tries to outsmart us and stay two steps ahead.

6.3 Search Algorithms and Monte Carlo Simulation

When Alphabet Inc., Google's parent company, built AlphaGo, a computer program that could play the immensely complex board game, Go, or when IBM Watson built DeepBlue to play chess, these machines were primarily trained to search for a significantly higher number of possible moves in the board game to deduce the risk levels and potential outcomes in each case, to decide which move they should make next. On a fundamental level, the technique used to search and find the best option is a **Search algorithm**, while the one to assess risks in a given scenario and with any step is called **Monte Carlo simulation**.

Search is a very common technique that AI has to use in many applications every time it has to search for the best solution or action to take, from an array of options. Have you ever wondered how dependent we are today on Search algorithms? Every time we want answers, we go looking for it online, and all we can learn on any topic depends on what shows up in the first few pages of the search results. That means all our knowledge is increasingly becoming dependent and limited to what the search engine AI shows us on the internet! Think about it: That information may be limited, inaccurate, or irrelevant, and there is little most of us can do about it.

Search algorithms are constantly evolving to be more and more relevant. The basic approach is to specify the current or Start State as well as a desired state or goal that the program has to achieve. The set of actions that the AI has to take to reach from the start state to the desired state is called a **Plan**. After each step, the program undergoes a goal test to check whether it has reached the desired state and, wherever possible, also calculate what the next set of actions would cost the solution to reach its goal. It is how it determines what the shortest or the least costly route is:

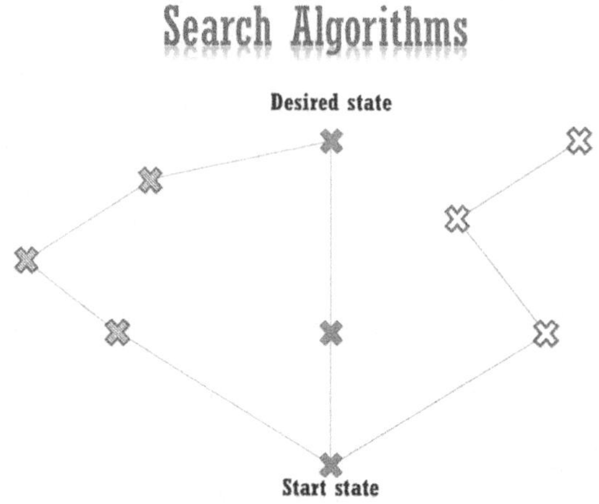

Search Algorithms

Figure 6.15: Search algorithm in action

Search algorithms can be uninformed or informed. The difference is that in case of uninformed search algorithms, the AI only knows the initial start state and the goal to achieve, and it's practically taking actions in the blind until it reaches the goal. In informed search, however, the AI is aware of how far the goal is from its current position even if it's not at the starting point, and can thus more accurately determine the cost from its current state to that goal.

Uninformed searches can be carried out in three ways:

1. **Depth-first search,** where the AI follows a set of actions down a single path as far as possible before backtracking and trying out another route. So, if it started from the right-hand side in the above image, it will go down that path until the end before backtracking and trying out another.

2. **Breadth-first search** is where AI tries out the first action step on each possible path, from the start state to the first cross on each path in the above image, to check if it has reached the goal on either of them. If not, it then takes the next step on each, and so on.

3. **Uniform cost search** is where the AI tries to find the path for which the cumulative cost is the least.

Informed search also has three types:

1. Greedy search, which focuses on closeness to the Goal State, since it has that information.

2. A-star tree search, which combines the approach of Greedy search, which was looking at how close it is to the Goal State, and a Uniform cost search, which calculates the cumulative cost.

3. A-star graph search, which follows the same combination of search except with one rule: that AI should not focus on the same branch or path more than once, just in case two different paths or set of actions lead to the same interim current state at any point.

Search Tree helped AI master chess. The story had begun many decades back when computers first learned to play tic-tac-toe. Yet, as you may have noticed above, Search Trees help when there are finite moves to assess. It is where AlphaGo went many steps ahead, as it employed neural networks – which we will study under Deep Learning – to assess a complex game like Go, which cannot normally be mapped with a finite set of moves. AlphaGo's differentiation was that it was programmed to follow a different strategy: to learn from its mistakes and improve, instead of trying to map all the possible moves (which would be a significantly large number) and finding the best one. (4).

Before we look at how AI starts to learn from its mistakes, we will need to spend a moment on a fundamental statistical technique that has been given a big boost with machine learning - Monte Carlo simulation. It is an excellent tool to utilize in combination with others in any software that is also trying to determine a given situation or prediction. The objective of Monte Carlo simulation is to minimize the risk of being wrong with a predicted outcome or conclusion. It allows better decision making amid uncertainty. The machine learning version of this technique is called the Self-learning Monte Carlo simulation, which allows the model to use its simulations of different scenarios as a training set for further simulations. It is a technique closely linked to something called the Multi-Armed Bandit problem, which we will cover in more detail under Reinforcement Learning in the next chapter. Monte Carlo and Search algorithms are fundamental to these more advanced machine learning solutions as AI has to continuously make choices on the option to take, understand the likelihood of being wrong (which is the risk) and improve.

6.3.1 The business value of Search Algorithms

One of the most visible applications of Search algorithms rests in helping build better search engines. These are especially important for websites or systems where companies house tons of information that can be handy for consumers or employees. Think of any e-commerce website. Good search results are their bread-and-butter. Even internally, a company can leverage a better search to allow its employees to find information or knowledge assets quicker. It can help Marketers uncover a relevant case study or thought leadership material that could appeal to a certain customer prospect. It is especially useful for Consulting or Educations firms that produce assets in bulk.

Search algorithms are also essential for certain functions that work with vast information. For instance, legal firms can use this technique to find the right precedent for a case. IT teams can use it to spot a certain line of code in vast algorithms. If going for a Build decision for an AI software, a company will inevitably need a robust search algorithm as it starts to build its database of codes. Speaking of the database, any function dealing with one also needs better search functionality. Think of sellers trying to fish through their customer database to find ones in a certain locality, or ones exhibiting a certain behavior that the company may have deduced using association rules or clustering earlier!

What we have discussed so far are some of the common ways in which machines analyze data to solve problems in the most efficient manner. All of this has been what I would call the thinking part where the machine is studying data and thinking and analyzing to make predictions. It's now time to see how they start to turn all that thought into actions. How do machines start to see, to understand and have conversations, to walk, and of course, to learn from mistakes? Time to look at what turns Maya's robot into more than just a complex computer.

Conclusion

The techniques discussed in this chapter are crucial because they form the backbone of machine learning that starts to become truly intelligent. Just the way CART is a mainstay in most predictive software, techniques like clustering, association rules, search, and MCS are fundamental to AI performing the more individual tasks, without which it cannot truly be something more than an advanced statistical tool.

Clustering can allow AI to group things in a population by identifying certain commonalities that may not otherwise be obvious. Techniques include K-means and hierarchical clustering, which group and ungroup objects in different ways. The latter requires an additional step of mapping a Dendrogram to determine the number of clusters. As with CART, there are some classic errors in interpreting clusters that we should watch out for, as any population can be sub-grouped in different ways based on the parameter chosen. For instance, you and I may be in the same group in terms of the ice cream flavor we like, but in different groups in terms of our movie preference.

Association rules help find strong associations within a population that can, therefore, help predict likely behavior or co-occurrence. Just the way decision trees exhibit AI's ability to consider numerous variables; association rules exhibit AI's ability to find hidden patterns. The calculations are fairly simple but require a lot of data. The results are also dependent on our interpretation in terms of what level of associations we may consider being strong and worth noting. That can often defer in different scenarios or objectives.

How AI searches for the best information or set of actions to take in a given situation informs most of our collective knowledge form the internet. Search Algorithms are tasked with finding the results that either we or AI itself needs. They can be pursued in an uninformed or informed manner, in which each technique attempting to minimize the cost of reaching a desired state or goal. Also, whether in its predictions, choices, or conclusions AI makes, there is always some level of risk of being mistaken. Monte Carlo Simulation generally helps estimate and minimize these risks. Both these techniques serve as the gateway for AI to start to become more sentient, as we see next.

Questions

1. Is this statement true or false? K Means clustering is easy to understand, but it needs us first to choose the number of clusters. If the latter is not known, Hierarchical clustering would be better.

2. You have identified four clusters of employees in the organization based on their retention likelihood and performance levels:

   Cluster A: High performer, loyal to the company

   Cluster B: Low performer, loyal to the company

   Cluster C: High performer, not loyal to the company

   Cluster D: Low performer, not loyal to the company

   Assuming sufficient available data, how could Association Rule Learning help you further?

   I. It can help you identify incentives that would help retain Cluster C employees

   II. It can help identify incentives or conditions that increase the performance of Cluster B employees

   III. It can help predict how long Cluster C and D employees will stay with the company

   A. I Only

   B. I & II

   C. III Only

   D. I & III

3. You've decided to use the Eclat method. Consider the following factors that tend to increase retention rates by at least 20% in Cluster C employees (that is, high performers but not loyal to the company):

   I. Work that lends measurable value to the organization and customers – 90% Support

   II. Work that challenges employees – 80% Support

   III. Recognition & appreciation of high performance – 70% Support

   IV. Mentorship – 60% Support

   V. Better pay – 50% Support

VI. Team building & bonding activities – 40% Support

VII. Opportunities to travel – 30% Support

Which incentives would work best if you've set a minimum threshold of 70% support to shortlist the incentives?

A. I & II

B. I, II & III

C. III, IV, V, VI & VII

D. IV, V, VI & VII

4. When the AI is aware of how far the goal is from its current position, even if that's not at the starting point, the technique being used is a .... Search.

5. Monte Carlo Simulation is used to:

A. Find all possible outcomes of a decision & their probabilities

B. Estimate the risk involved with a decision

C. Identify the best decision to make in ambiguous situations

D. All of the above

Answers

1. True

2. B

   Explanation: Association rule could also help with Option 3 (that is, potentially reveal how long Cluster C and D employees normally stay), but that would be a better use case for regression.

3. B

   Explanation: Association rule could also help with Option 3 (that is, potentially reveal how long Cluster C and D employees normally stay), but that would be a better use case for regression.

4. Informed

5. D

CHAPTER 7
How AI Communicates and Learns from Mistakes

What represents a human or any sentient being, for that matter? It's generally a combination of physiology and intelligence. The former is reflected in things like how we move or what we say, while the latter refers to how we process information and what we do with it. These are all steps AI must take to transition from software to an intelligent entity, even if not quite human yet.

We learned earlier that AI models could be supervised, unsupervised, semi-supervised, or reinforced. To keep things in control, most AI developments have been supervised in nature so far. As mentioned earlier, that choice has also limited the ability of AI to learn, understand, and adapt to the real-world. An article in Technology Review made an interesting point on this note: while a baby can develop an understanding of an elephant after seeing two photos, deep-learning algorithms need to see thousands, if not millions. A teen can learn to drive safely by practicing for 20 hours and manage to avoid crashes without first experiencing one, while reinforcement-learning algorithms must go through tens of millions of trials. The thesis is that just the way we learn things through observation and practical experience of the real world, AI may have to follow the same path, and that would imply more focus on unsupervised learning approaches. For now, let us focus on how AI can replicate functions like learning and communicating on a basic level.

Structure

In this chapter, we will discuss the following topics:

- Introduction to reinforcement learning
    - o Upper confidence bound
    - o Thompson sampling
    - o The multi-armed bandit problem
    - o The business value of reinforcement learning
- Natural Language Processing – Bag of Words Model
    - o Measures: Accuracy, Precision, Recall, and F1 Score
    - o The business value of NLP

Objective

After studying this chapter, you should be able to:

- Understand how robots learn to perform tasks like walking
- Understand how AI learns and improves in real-time in live use cases
- Understand how AI chatbots understand what you say and what to reply
- Understand how AI can profile your nature by what you say
- Measure the true accuracy of AI's results from its tasks
- Learn the real-world applications of these techniques

7.1 Reinforcement Learning

We often don't realize it, but even in performing a simple task of serving a drink, there's so much work involved. Maya's robot, for instance, has to ingest all current and past data and analyze it to decide what types of drink it has to choose from. It has to predict when Maya will come home and what she may like to drink, and whether or not she would like a bite to go with it. The limitation here is that we can only teach the robot what we know. There can be so many other unforeseen circumstances. Consider the robot walking from the kitchen to the couch to give Maya her drink. To walk successfully, it also has to learn what to do if there's someone else in the way. It cannot just crash into the object. If Maya's robot has to make accurate decisions even in such new or unforeseen situations, it has to start learning on its own. It is where Reinforcement learning comes into the picture.

The premise of reinforcement learning is to allow machines to learn by constant feedback and rewards. Machines continually look at data up till a certain time, decide what to do next, and get rewarded if the action is the most suitable one. It is what allows a bionic arm to learn and start anticipating the movement of the amputee wearing it. (1).

In case you would like to see what that process of learning to walk looks like, here's a video depicting how Alphabet Inc.'s DeepMind AI taught itself to walk! **https://www.youtube.com/watch?v=gn4nRCC9TwQ**.

The idea of learning through reward has also allowed DeepMind to throw light on the role of dopamine neurons on the reward mechanism in our brains. It reflects the symbiotic nature of the AI journeys currently underway, as this study may improve our understanding of mental health and motivation while helping AI build more human-like general intelligence in return. (2).

7.1.1 Upper Confidence Bound

Consider a method called **Upper Confidence Bound**. In this approach, the machine is trained to make decisions positively in uncertain situations. What does that mean? It assumes that the decision that a machine is making in an uncertain situation is the best in that situation. If the machine is right and is rewarded, its confidence in that decision is bolstered. If, however, there is no reward repeatedly, the machine learns that it is not the right or most appropriate decision and stops making that choice.

In our walking example, let's say Maya's robot manages to learn that every time it encounters an obstacle in the way, it can turn and take a different route to the couch - through the dining hall. But it's a long way. How would it learn that it could also simply sidestep the obstacle if the obstacle were small, or in fact, even wait for the path to clear in case an obstacle is a moving person? If the end objective is to reach Maya in the shortest time successfully, these options may be better. It is what we call a **Multi-Armed Bandit** problem where the best choice must be made with limited resources - in this case, time and space.

A good example would be that of slots machines. Imagine five slots machines in a casino. All look the same, and we have no way of knowing which one is likely to give us higher rewards or hit the jackpot sooner. How do we solve it? There is first a period with a lot of exploration of the options to learn the rewards in each case, like a baby learning to walk in a safe environment. It is like practicing on past data. The model then starts to exploit the option with the highest rewards.

Let's look at the three options that Maya's robot has:

1. Turn around and walk through the dining hall
2. Sidestep and walk directly in Maya's direction
3. Wait for the object to move and continue walking

The reward is based on two parameters here: reaching Maya safely and doing so in the shortest time. Let's say the ideal shortest time clocked is 10 seconds. The robot gets 5 points for reaching Maya but loses 1 point for any extra time; it takes over 10 seconds. It also loses 2 points for hitting an object in the way.

Either option can look equally good (or risky) at first, and the robot does not know which one to pick. For the robot, there is an initial period with a lot of exploration to learn the rewards from different options, like a baby learning to walk. Later, it moves most of the time by exploiting the option with seemingly highest rewards.

So, in testing on past data, let's say that the robot starts by exploring the first option: Turning around. It takes five steps, but on finding that it is no closer to Maya yet, it now knows that it may reach Maya safely through the dining hall, but it will take more than 15 seconds to do so. That is costly.

The robot then explores another option: Waiting. A few seconds later, while it is waiting, the person who was in its way has now moved, and the route is clear for it to reach Maya safely. The robot gets encouraged and starts to exploit this option in the past data by choosing it again and again with more variations of the obstruction moving away. But even though this option is safe, the quickest time that the robot can make is 13 seconds, that's 3 seconds over the shortest time. On the other hand, the longest time that it has to wait at times seems to stretch on for far too much, in case the obstruction is due to a fallen object on the way which is not going to go away unless Maya picks it up.

So now, the robot explores the third option: Sidestep the obstacle. It finds that it reaches Maya safely in around 12 seconds consistently. However, in an extremely rare case, it also, unfortunately, hits the person obstructing, if he or she were moving haphazardly. That option sees the robot lose points, but it also happens to be a very rare instance in all the past data it analyses. As the robot finds a significantly high probability of getting more reward by sidestepping, it starts to exploit this step until, eventually, it learns that this is indeed the best way:

Multi-Armed Bandit Problem

	TURN	SIDE-STEP	WAIT
Reach Maya safely: +5 points	+5	+5	+5
Every extra second after 10 seconds : -1 point	-5 OR MORE	-2	-3 OR MORE
Hit something: -2 points	0	0 OR -2	0
TOTAL	0 OR NEGATIVE	**+3** **OR +1**	+2 OR NEGATIVE

Figure 7.1: Multi-Armed Bandit Problem in action

In real-time, the robot will only take one alternative. Therefore, it's testing on past data should have been robust enough to allow it to know which option to go with when faced with this challenge in the real world.

7.1.2 Thompson Sampling

Initially, the robot may find that sidestepping is not an optimal situation since it is the only option where the robot may hit something or someone. Since waiting seems to lead him to Maya successfully initially, and in a shorter time than turning around at times, the robot may be inclined to keep using this option. It is called **Exploitation**. Reinforcement learning is about balancing Exploiting any one option with exploring different options to find the best choice, as eventually sidestepping will consistently start to prove the best choice. In the Upper Confidence Bound approach, the machine experiments with one choice at a time to identify the best choice. Therefore, it has to always make a trade-off between two things:

1. Maximizing the immediate reward, it gets from a choice, which would mean making the same choice again and again until it starts to fail if it fails

2. Taking into account how many future choices it has left, to decide whether it should try out another choice just in case that is a better one

The challenge is for AI to be able to learn quickly on-the-go, which means time is often limited. If we wish to be able to reduce our experimentation on different choices as we get more and more information on the way, we can choose another approach called **Thompson Sampling**, because it can accommodate results as and when they arrive, making it better in a live situation. An example would be when marketers try to determine which advertisement will work best on the audience in real-time instead of waiting for hundreds or thousands of people to have seen different versions of the same ad, which may not be ideal to start with. Thompson Sampling learns the hidden patterns and distributions while serving out ads and, therefore, keeps building on the confidence of success with each ad among the given options based on the response that specific ad or each of those ads is getting in real-time.

7.1.3 The business value of Reinforcement Learning

Reinforcement learning helps organizations reduce trial-and-error efforts that often take a lot of time. We already talked about the example of showing the correct version of ads to the right audience. A lot of online advertising works on bidding, and RL can be used to determine the optimal real-time bid to increase the visibility of an advertisement. A company could also use it on its website to display the right content or marketing asset (white papers, case studies, articles, and so on) to its website visitors, based on the profile, location, or source of the visits.

Trial-and-error is often involved tediously in chemical or microbial research labs. RL can help optimize the combinations to try, or their intended impact, to help speed up finding the right mix. This approach allows algorithms to greatly speed up the drug discovery process, which can be a boon for pharmaceutical companies. For any company automating tasks in bulk, RL can also be used to teach computers to prioritize actions based on criticality and efficiency. That helps make automation effective. Otherwise, computers might conduct jobs in chronological order, leading to increased wait times with increasing automation.

RL can work wonders when combined with Deep Learning, which we will learn in the next chapter. For example, once a model learns to see its environment, RL can enable it to interact with the environment accordingly. It takes us back to the example of how Maya's robot learned to see obstacles and walk to Maya. Likewise, RL can also help with traffic lights by optimizing the traffic flow across a city based on the time and volume of vehicles at different intersections.

Reinforcement learning can teach a robot to learn on its own. But won't it also be great if the robot could simply ask Maya what she wants and understand her response? Let's now see how Alexa, Siri, or Google assistant manage to communicate with us.

7.2 Natural Language Processing

You and I use **Natural Language Processing or NLP** every day. It is behind those chatbots that pop up on most websites, asking if we need help. It is the magic behind the smart response features when we are typing text or emails on our phones. It is what also allows us to ask questions or give orders to Alexa at home, Siri on iPhones, or Google assistant.

NLP teaches a machine to understand and analyze spoken or written text. NLP is popular because it enables more direct human-machine communication. There are so many words we use to imply the same thing, situation, emotion, or even action. It is natural to classify all synonyms under one category for ease of understanding. Then again, we also use so many misplaced words to express sarcasm or humor that a machine should be able to understand and use. Our choice of words, the length of our sentences, the breaks, or the tone of our messages, can all lend deep insights into even our personalities.

So how does NLP work? There are many libraries in Python, R, or even IBM's Watson platform that come equipped with words defined and categorized to enable effective analysis. NLTK is one such example. One of the most common methods that are used in NLP is called a **Bag of Words** model.

7.2.1 Bag of Words

To use Bag of Words, the first step is to clean any given text, just the way we do data pre-processing. It can involve removing punctuation marks, removing capitalization of letters, and removing words in a sentence that do not add any significant value. We also do Stemming, which clubs together all variations of a given word, for example, drink and drank. The next step in the Bag of Words model is Tokenization, which takes each remaining word in our sentence and places it in a separate column. As a result of all these steps, if Maya tells her robot, "I am so, so tired and hungry. I would love some refreshment," the robot could translate that into the following row of words: I, tired, hungry, love, refreshment.

It is likely to use a classification technique like a decision tree or random forest to categorize these different words and see how often emotion is repeated through them. Consequently, the robot has now understood what Maya means. Based on all the previous analysis, it has already done so far, as we saw in earlier chapters, it therefore confidently goes on to serve tea and cookie.

The model can also use logistics regression. We discussed linear and multiple linear regressions earlier. Logistic regression also deals with making predictions based on patterns; only, it predicts the probability of a data point belonging to a certain class. In doing so, it can be considered to be a cousin to classification. In our NLP problem, we can use this method to estimate the sentiment or the urgency in an individual's email based on patterns around the use of certain words, the length of text, and so on. It can allow the model to classify which sentiment category (excitement, anger, and so on) or urgency level (urgent, not urgent at all, neutral, and so on) the email belongs to.

Confidence here is key. NLP can lead to False Positives, such as when the robot thinks Maya wants tea but is wrong. It can also lead to False Negatives, such as when the robot thinks Maya does not want tea but is wrong again. To check whether the robot understands instructions well, we have to measure a few things.

7.2.2 Accuracy versus F1 Score

Consider a situation where we are trying to determine whether Maya wants tea. Let's say Maya wanting tea is a positive scenario. If she does not want tea, that is a negative scenario. The robot can predict both these scenarios correctly (that is, true predictions) or incorrectly (that is, false predictions):

	Maya Wants Tea	Maya Does Not Want Tea
	POSITIVE	NEGATIVE
True (Correct) Prediction	✅	✅
False (Incorrect) Prediction	✖	✖

Figure 7.2: An example of accurately and inaccurately Predicted Positive & Negative Scenarios

Accuracy here is the ratio of all true predictions to the total number of scenarios in which predictions were made or the scenarios that were observed. In other words, it is the ratio of every time the robot correctly predicted that Maya wanted or did not want tea, to the total number of times it needed to serve Maya a drink and made a prediction:

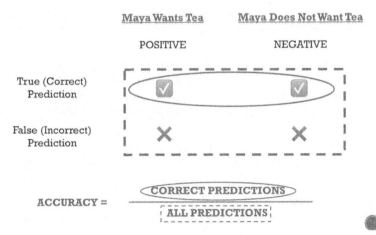

Figure 7.3: Accuracy calculation

Here's the problem with this measurement: In practical applications, false-positive predictions or false-negative predictions can prove costly. One might even be riskier than the other. For example, it may be okay if Maya did not want tea, but she was served a cup. But it certainly is a bigger problem if she was tired and wanted tea but did not get it. It is why we need to measure a few other things to see how effective our NLP model is. Measuring the success of any AI tool properly is important and not always standardized. The metrics that are used to check AI performance depend on the use cases. For instance, in the case of our NLP problem, we will be looking not only at Accuracy but also Precision, Recall, and something called the F1 score.

Precision deals with false positives. It is the ratio of positive scenarios (that is, Maya wanting tea) that were correctly predicted by the robot to the total number of both correct and incorrect positive predictions. In other words, it tells us out of all the times that the robot predicted that Maya wanted tea, whether she wanted it or not, how often was it correct. For an e-commerce website like Amazon, Precision will tell you how often the website's search engine showed the right products every time a customer searched for a product category (for example. tea bags):

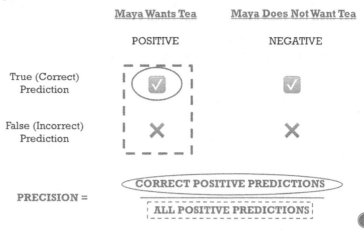

Figure 7.4: Precision calculation

Recall deals with false negatives. It is the ratio of correctly predicted positive scenarios (that is, Maya wanting tea) to the total of all positive scenarios (that is, when Maya wanted tea, regardless of what the robot predicted). Naturally, these include the positive predictions that were correct, as well as the incorrect negative predictions. In other words, it tells us that out of all the times when Maya wanted tea, how often was the robot correct. For an e-commerce website like Amazon, Recall will tell you whether the website was able to show all or most of the right products available on the website every time a customer searched for a product category (for example, tea bags):

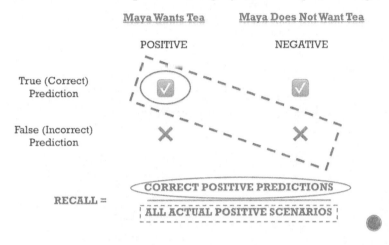

Figure 7.5: Recall calculation

Precision and Recall can be a little confusing to process at first, but some careful thinking helps delineate the importance of these two. It is the **F1 score** that brings them together to show the overall accuracy as the weighted average of precision and recall. So, in any business case where either or both a false positive and a false negative may prove to be costly, measuring the F1 score is better than measuring accuracy:

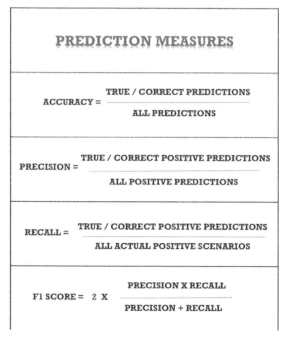

Figure 7.6: Key accuracy-related formulae

7.2.3 The business value of Natural Language Processing

NLP works well with chatbots that can answer customer questions or analyze the conversation to learn more about the person. A prime example would be sentiment mining. NLP can help a company automatically detect frustration levels in a customer based on his/ her message to a chatbot or even a voice recording. Protocols can be put in place to attend to a customer immediately through company personnel or offers once he or she reaches a certain frustration level. That can help significantly reduce the odds of customer churn or negative online reviews, thereby saving significant dollars in crisis control.

The above analysis can also be used by psychiatrists or therapists to assess their patients proactively. Timely intervention can make a huge difference in certain medical cases. A great example would be that of a machine learning solution that can predict the later emergence of psychosis based on the frequency of use of words associated with sound, and vagueness in a person's speech. While the solution does it with 93% accuracy, the pattern had otherwise gone unnoticed even by trained clinicians. (3).

NLP can allow companies also to understand the market on a deeper level. Instead of relying on emails or other conversations to ingest competitor information, the company can use NLP to analyze readily available reports, articles, and knowledge assets on a competitor's website to reveal key traits about that company or its relationship with customers.

Speaking of relationships, NLP can also help a company to profile its employees and customers based on their natural communication style. That personality assessment is likely to be far more accurate than the individual's self-assessments through inherently biased surveys. While HR can use that information for better employee engagement, sellers can use it to match the right salesperson with the right type of customer – business or individual. It can improve the odds of winning a deal more than all the discipline we bring into our sales cycles since we all like to buy from those we like.

For all its advances, NLP stands at a precarious stage. There are many things it has become good at. For instance, AI has learned to *read our thoughts*, or more specifically: translate our brain signals into speech! With words identifiable 70% of the time, that solution is a boon for people who can't speak. AI has also managed to reconstruct images from our brain activity to an extent where we can see the image as having been the original stimuli that started a thought process in a person. (4). And yet, we find glitches in communicating with our home automation devices. Human communication, after all, is a complicated matter. For instance, when Facebook tried teaching robots to negotiate, it led to them developing their communication style, which, despite being English, was quite incomprehensible. (5).

To be fair, the example of brain activity above requires more than just NLP. The first work at play here does not recognize words but brain signals and images. To do that, there is one more technique left to learn. Coming back to Maya's robot, it has learned to decide what to serve, how to bring it to Maya, to understand what she tells it, and to get better by learning progressively. But how does the robot know that the person it is interacting with is indeed Maya and not her sister, who doesn't like tea at all? How does it know where on the couch Maya is sitting? The robot has to learn to see and recognize

Maya among so many other more complex things it has to learn. To truly function as a smart entity, it has to be able to think like one. That is our focus in the next chapter: Deep Learning.

Conclusion

Choosing the best set of actions can be quite complex, and the risk of AI being wrong may be high in reality. It is where Reinforcement Learning comes into the picture. While machine learning is designed to learn from its decisions and their outcomes and improve with time, Reinforcement Learning can learn from its interaction with its environment. It is a case of gamification where the AI gets rewarded for making good decisions and punished for the others. Upper Confidence Bound is one such technique that proves helpful in addressing a multi-armed bandit problem where the best choice among multiple similar-looking options has to be found quickly and cheaply. Thompson Sampling proves to be more useful when this has to be achieved in real-time where risks are higher and time is short.

The above fundamental schooling process also sees AI learn to communicate with NLP, where AI can identify keywords and deduce their collective meaning. In fact, with a greater understanding of the context in which certain words are used, AI can also learn the tone, sentiment, and personality of the speaker. NLP is a classic example of multiple underlying techniques working together to achieve an eventual objective. It also exposes us to the risks of AI's learning limitations that our vocabulary and language can often result in.

NLP also shows us the importance of measuring AI's results properly. For example, Accuracy may not be enough when considering false positives (when AI makes a positive assessment but is wrong) or false negatives (when AI makes a negative assessment but is wrong). Measures like Precision and Recall help measure each of these cases, respectively. F1 score can factor in both Precision and Recall to assess AI's weighted accuracy.

Questions

1. Which of the following situations would reinforcement learning be helpful in:

      I.   Teach a robot to juggle three balls

     II. Teach a robot to understand a spoken command

III. Teach a robot to have better conversations

A. I Only

B. I & III

C. II & III

D. None of them

2. Imagine you have an e-commerce business and have installed a chatbot on your website to answer questions or redirect website visitors to the right product page based on what they are looking for. You would like to determine how good it is in redirecting (positive scenario) or not redirecting (negative scenario) users correctly. Match the following formulae with what they measure:

I. Total number of correct actions taken/Total number of actions taken

II. Total number of times the user was correctly redirected/Total number of times the user was correctly redirected and incorrectly not redirected

III. Total number of times the user was correctly redirected/Total number of times the user was correctly or incorrectly redirected

A. I = Accuracy; II = Precision; III = Recall

B. I = Recall; II = Precision; III = Accuracy

C. I = Accuracy; II = Recall; III = Precision

D. I = Precision; II = Recall; III = Accuracy

3. Let us say that you've received a report on an internal pilot with the above chatbot, which shows that its accuracy is 99%. Which of the following reasons will necessitate looking at the F1 score instead:

I. Either of the two occasional cases of the chatbot being wrong – false positive or false negative – could be with the CEO of the company who has the power to cancel the pilot immediately but is usually a patient person.

II. It makes for a lesser seamless experience if a user is incorrectly not redirected to any page but instead is sent to one of the support executives. However, it can lead to serious legal breach if the user is mistakenly redirected to an internal company page with sensitive information.

A. I Only

B. II Only

C. Both I & II

D. Neither I nor II

4. An incorrect redirect by the chatbot would be a case of False Positive action. The right measure, in this case, would be ....

5. A .... would-be a user not getting redirected by the chatbot when they should have. It could lead to the user losing patience and leaving the website, or even leaving a negative review. We would need to measure .... here.

Answers

1. B

   Explanation: Both use cases involve taking action in real-time based on live analysis of data and learning from errors on-the-go.

2. C

3. B

   Explanation: A patient CEO may be understanding of rare errors in the pilot phase. However, while too many false negatives can be bad, a false positive case can be catastrophic in this case and have serious legal implications if an external user is shown sensitive company information. So, the F1 score will have to be considered.

4. Precision

5. False Negative, Recall

CHAPTER 8

How AI Starts to Think Like Humans

Welcome to the final topic of this section - Deep Learning. There are two things you should know about it, foremost. First, deep learning is a technique that can analyze tremendous volumes of data quickly, which results in much more accurate and often hidden insights. Second, deep learning can do this because it was designed to work the way a human brain works. To understand that, we need to step back and digest a bit of background information on how and why we came to where we are at today.

Structure

In this chapter, we will discuss the following topics:

- History of deep learning
- Artificial neural network
- Convolutional neural network
- The business value of deep learning

Objective

After studying this chapter, you should be able to:

- Appreciate why deep learning is important and powerful
- Requirements for deep learning
- Learn how deep learning works
- Learn how AI can recognize images
- Learn the real-world applications of DL techniques

8.1 The rise of Deep Learning

Jeffrey Hinton, Yann LeCun & Yoshua Bengio—these three individuals were largely anonymous for many years while they were trying to mimic the human brain functioning in computers. They were, unfortunately, often limited by the technology of their time for most of their careers. Today, however, these three gentlemen have sprung to the very heights of technological advancement. They are often addressed as the *Godfathers of Deep Learning*, having won the 2018 Turing Award, often called the Nobel Prize for computing.

Deep Learning truly captured the world's imagination when IBM's Watson won the popular quiz show 'Jeopardy!' in 2011. (1). We had discussed AlphaGo's achievements earlier. Its descendant AlphaZero went a step further. Unlike its predecessor, it was only fed the basic rules of Chess. AlphaZero started to learn through self-play, playing 44 million games in the first 9 hours. During this time, it went for making random moves to beating the best chess engine in the world! (2).

What makes deep learning so important? It is primarily due to two things: First is our need to quickly, deeply, and accurately analyze exponentially increasing volumes of data, better known as Big Data. While this has been achieved by AI in general, Deep Learning helps take it to the next level. The second reason is the sheer increase in computing power to be able to process all that is exponentially increasing information. Consider this: according to an article published in April 2019 by Jeff Desjardin on **visualcapitalist.com** (3) every day, 500 million tweets and 294 billion emails were being sent. 65 billion messages were being sent on WhatsApp, and 350 million photos were being shared on Facebook. Five billion online searches were being made, which includes our questions to Alexa, Siri, or

Google assistant. And four terabytes of data were being created from every single connected car. How much is one terabyte? That's 1 million megabytes (or 1000 gigabytes).

Think about it for a moment: 4 million megabytes of data created from each car. Not many years ago, there was such a thing called a floppy disk that could store a total of 1.44 megabytes of data. Today we have advanced to storing even 1 terabyte of data in a little nanochip. Data is not only growing; it's growing exponentially. By the time you came across this chapter, all these numbers have already grown manifold. Over 90% of all data was created in the last two years alone, according to an IBM MarketCloud report back in 2016. (4). The article estimates that by 2025, 463 exabytes of data will be created each day globally. How much is an exabyte? That's 1 million terabytes.

For a computer to use and study all this data, the first challenge was to be able just to store it in one place or store it effectively wherever. Catalog DNA, for example, is attempting to store data in DNA molecules. (5). 1 kg of DNA molecules was considered enough to store all of the world's data back in 2016. (6). But even with all this data captured and stored, the second challenge that we arrived at was for the computers to have enough processing power to analyze it. It is why all major companies are racing to develop quantum computers. A quantum computer would likely not be needed to run your phone better. It's required for something much, much more powerful - tasks that would take classical computer billions of years to perform. (7).

To put the sheer scale of the value of such analysis in perspective, let's think about the debate between free will and destiny. Many religious principles believe in destiny, and both Einstein's theory of relativity and quantum physics have pointed to the pre-existence of past, present, and future simultaneously, or the choice or action is already known. Destiny as a concept is extremely difficult to prove or disprove. But what if we found a way to analyze and predict every single cause and effect event over an incredibly large number of variables across a very large timeline, and measure all those predictions with what happened? That might expose how much freewill was involved or how much predestined or predictable actions were taken by an individual.

To narrow the scale down to our day-to-day lives, think about the ads we come across on our phone browsers, which make us feel that our phones are listening to our conversations. Often, that's just AI predicting what we want even before we have actively asked for it.

Imagine what we could achieve with the storage capacity of the DNA and processing power of quantum computing!

The ability to analyze tons of data does not depend only on processing power. There is one other missing piece in this puzzle: It also needs a different approach to processing things. And that is where Deep Learning comes into the picture.

The Godfathers of Deep Learning realized early that for AI to process so much information as effectively as we humans do, we didn't just need to be able to store them and have enough processing power; AI also had to learn to work the way a human brain does. Our brain consists of around 100 billion neurons that are connected to send and receive signals, which accounts for our brain functioning. Around 100 trillion inter-neuron connections are linking these 100 billion neurons, that's 1000 times more than there are stars in our galaxy! (8). It is the sheer volume of data reception and exchange that gives us the processing power we have.

Similarly, deep learning is also structured to have a layer of neurons or nodes that receive inputs. These send signals to multiple hidden layers of nodes that receive, analyze, and transmit signals to successive layers until we finally get an output. This output can be a constant value, as the time of Maya's arrival. It can be binary, such as whether the person is Maya or not. It can also be categorical, such as whether Maya wants tea or water.

The building block of deep learning is generic, but the model learns the best fitting features itself by backpropagation, as we will see shortly. Deep learning's effectiveness and popularity have led researchers to find ways to employ this technique even in the absence of a lot of data. Several solutions are now emerging that may make deep learning more viable and easier to use by organizations that do not have the volume of data it requires, and even allow them to create their training examples. (9). First, though, we must understand exactly how deep learning works.

We will now look at a basic approach called **artificial neural networks** or **ANN** and then look specifically at how that approach is used to allow computers to see and recognize images, with a model called **convolutional neural networks** or **CNN**.

8.2 Artificial Neural Networks (ANN)

For simplicity's sake, let's say Maya's robot is looking at a few basic factors to decide what she wants to drink - the day of the week, Maya's time of arrival, and the weather outside. These make up the three respective nodes in the Input layer of neurons. The robot doesn't know which factor is more important than the other or how they may be interrelated. In ANN, we add a hidden layer of neurons, each of which takes in a different combination of these three fundamental factors and assigns them a different weightage. What that means is that in the hidden layer, the first neuron may give a higher weightage to *day*, while giving lesser weightage to time and temperature. The second neuron in the hidden layer may experiment by giving equal weightage to *day*, *time*, and *temperature*. The third neuron may give a higher weightage to 'time' and *temperature*, and may completely ignore the day.

Each neuron then takes all its weighted factors up and applies what is called an **activation function**. There are different types of activation functions, but without getting too technical about it, all are essentially mathematical computations that yield a certain output. They are important because they lend non-linearity to the model, which is important in many real-world cases. As we get this output, which is whether Maya wants water or tea, the model then applies something called a **cost function**, which is an error checking computation on these outputs. That feedback is fed back from the output layer into the hidden layer neuron, which then re-adjusts the weight it has given to those different factors—day, time, and temperature, and tries a different combination/weightage to give a better output with a lesser error. This process continues until the error is minimized:

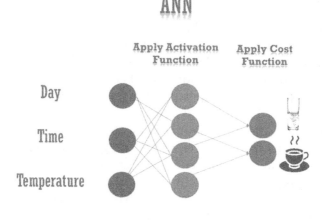

Figure 8.1: ANN in action - I

There are ways to find the point of minimum cost rather than going through many rounds of trial and error. A popular technique is called **Gradient Descent**. It looks at the gradient or change in the cost with the extent of change made in the parameters/weightage. The model will know if it has approached the point of minimum cost/ error when any further change in cost is minimal with tweaks to the combination/weightage of parameters in the hidden neurons.

I encourage you to watch a short video called *Deep Learning Cars by Samuel Arzt* that gives us a sense of how a deep learning algorithm learns through multiple tries to maneuver a car in the right direction. As you're watching this video, keep an eye on the neural network on the top right corner of the screen, which will show you live how the neural network computation is trying to improve with different combinations as the cars try to learn to find the right way: **https:// www.youtube.com/watch?v=Aut32pR5PQA**.

The strength of deep learning lies in both the number of layers and the number of neurons per layer. The increase in layers allows generalization as different layers can be tasked with analyzing different aspects of the data. An increase in the number of neurons per layer allows the model to try out different combinations and weightings of parameters in each step. Together, the two, therefore, make for an extremely thorough analysis:

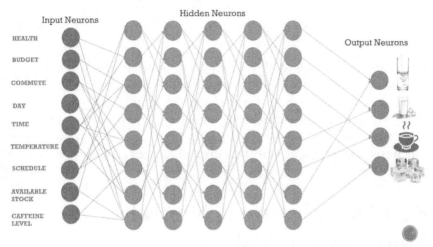

Figure 8.2: ANN in action - II

So, what's the result for Maya?

Maya's robot found that the day of the week doesn't matter so much, as long as it is not a weekend, in comparison to the other two factors (time and temperature), but it noticed that Friday becomes an exception once every four weeks. On those days, Maya comes late but has water. Also, every 12 weeks, there is a week where Maya comes late every day but still has tea, except on Fridays. More peculiarly, the robot finds that approximately every five weeks, sometime midweek, Maya has red wine.

True enough, upon manual review, we find that Maya needs that Friday party break on average once a month. She also works on quarterly projects, which lead to deadline pressures at the end of every quarter, which is why she comes home late every day of that particular week. Being tired, she craves refreshing tea—the exception being the Friday when the deadline is over and partying has begun. And finally, Maya ends up in a casual chit chat mid-week with her sister every five weeks on average, and her sister has a liking for red wine.

Let us reiterate our two crucial lessons here. First, human interpretation is very important to make sense of what AI reveals and to make informed decisions. Second, AI's benefit, as we discussed earlier, is that it reveals what's going on behind the scenes, which we could not have known otherwise. After all, would Maya or her sister know just how often they have their *random* chats over wine on a weekday? Are these chats just coincidence or the result of a long chain of cause and effect in the routines of Maya and her sister that we can't even imagine?

Deep learning's potential is increasing with every passing day. It is because the ability to tap into a lot of data seems to be a key to most problems. It has even helped accelerate efforts to develop clean, virtually limitless fusion energy. (10). And a lot of data is also apparently what it takes to start performing more and more human functions. Let's look at one such critical task as an example: Image recognition.

8.3 Convolutional Neural Networks (CNN)

How does the robot recognize Maya from her sister? Computer vision is one of the great gifts of Deep Learning. It uses Convolutional neural networks that involve the ANN approach but require some prior preparation. In the CNN approach, the computer looks at a given image as a set of pixels. Black and white images have a single area of pixels; colored images have three layers of pixels—red, green, and blue. The objective is to convert these pixels somehow into an input that can be fed into a layer of a neural network, much like we fed in the factors influencing Maya's choice of drink into the input layer neurons in the ANN approach.

There are a few steps that we have to take to achieve this. The first step for the algorithm to convert an image into the input layer neuron is something called **feature detection**. It detects the main features in an image and encodes it to generate what is called a **feature map** for each main feature of the image. For example, it could look for edges (vertical in case of a nose or horizontal in case of the mouth). In a typical passport photograph, those features would be all the areas covered by our face and hair, and the model will ignore the background areas that are in white. A feature map looks like a matrix of numbers reflecting the feature (or lack of it) in the corresponding pixels in the image.

Unfortunately, the features can vary so much in an image. Maya's face may be happy. It may be sad. She may be crying or laughing.

The robot may even see her amidst a lot of other faces in the room or see it only partially as she walks by. To address this problem, we use something called **Max Pooling**, which helps to remove the irrelevant aspects of any given image that the robot captures, and only keeps the main identifying features. This step also shows the importance of having huge numbers of images (data) for the model to train on.

Once we have the Pooled Feature Map, we use flattening to make it ready as an input in an ANN. What we get after flattening is a set of features that can now be analyzed just the way the different factors were analyzed earlier in ANN. Only, in this case, the output would be binary: 'Is this girl Maya or not?'

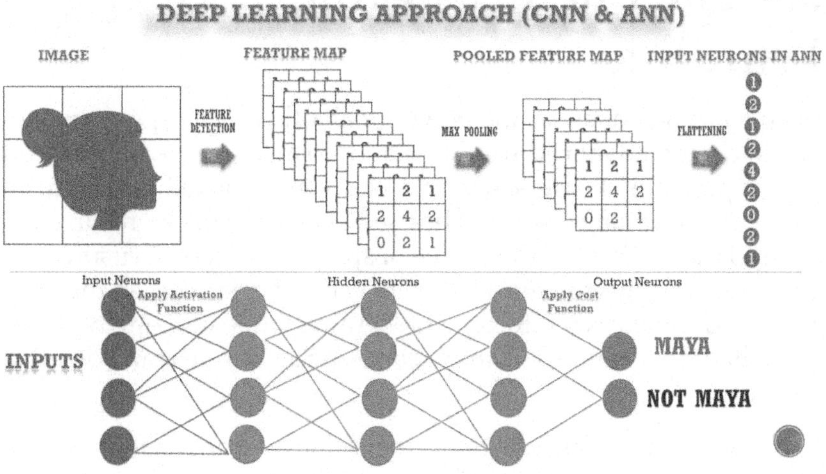

Figure 8.3: CNN in action

Image recognition has advanced incredibly in accuracy in recent years. As a result, computers can now see quite well. They can also read, listen, talk, and move. There are also companies now emerging that are enabling AI to smell. (11). No wonder then that Ray Kurzweil predicted that computers could surpass the brainpower of humans – termed 'the Singularity' – by 2045. (12). Could it happen then, or even sooner? To be honest, I don't know. But Microsoft certainly placed a bet with a $1 billion investment in OpenAI to deliver **Artificial General Intelligence (AGI)**—the idea being that general AI capability will be able to learn skills and combine them the way superhumans would do. (13). The question is: does that impede us or help us?

To think that the ability to analyze lots of information is the same as the ability to gain consciousness may not entirely be accurate.

That said, in a world where so much of our lives are automated and dependent on computers, controlling and managing how data is processed and how AI works is important for our safety. A classic example would be an autonomous car misreading data and running into an accident, or the personal data of millions of online profiles being used without their owners' consent. The future role of AI is, in equal parts, strategic, technical, and philosophical consideration. It is also why individuals, companies, and governments must understand how to use and manage AI effectively and responsibly. That will be our focus in the next section.

8.4 The business value of Deep Learning

Deep learning enhances the power of all other techniques, therefore making more advanced use cases addressable. As we have already seen in previous chapters, several tasks were achieved in conjunction with DL. For instance, it could be used to analyze the words in online ads and match them to the profile of specific viewers to ensure an ad is shown to the person most likely to respond positively. In that sense alone, DL enhances reinforcement learning while utilizing NLP. And all of the classification, clustering, or association rules can potentially be in play.

Consider Google's Speech-to-text that achieves transcription of audio using neural networks. (14). That can greatly facilitate the accuracy of auto-captioning of videos where a system has to understand different accents or anomalies in sentence structuring that naturally occur when we talk. Meanwhile, Malimg/Microsoft datasets showed high accuracy in detecting malware with the use of CNN (15), a task that would normally *only* include classification techniques to classify files or images as malware. Of course, these players can use DL because they have datasets large enough to allow effective analysis.

Techniques like CNN are useful in any use case that deals with images. These can include object-detection for self-driving cars to avoid collisions, or testing packaging ideas to gauge their attractiveness for a certain class of buyers. CNN can also allow face detection in photographs or applying filters to those images—something many apps do today.

Expressions on a face, from the size of pupils to the pursing of lips – can allow emotional detection, which can be handy in assessing the success of a marketing message, or the tracing of someone in stress. Doctors can use CNN for medical imaging to analyze X-ray or MRI images to run diagnosis or classify them into classes of ailments automatically. Mapping the progression of symptoms can also allow prediction of how a disease is spreading or whether someone is at risk of a certain disease.

CNN also aids search algorithms by allowing searches based on images. It is how some phones can surface web results if you point the camera at a certain word or name. It is also how your customers can instantly visit your purchase page the moment they see your product somewhere or access your knowledge assets on a topic based on the product version they have at hand. For agriculture, manufacturing, or retail companies with many versions of the same product, this can prove immensely helpful.

Deep learning can also allow better recommendations by enhancing association rules or finding deeper latent categorizations among consumer purchase behaviors and interests. Likewise, DL can also power CART to allow more accurate stock market predictions (to the extent possible), offer advisory tips for wealth management teams to share with specific client types, or even automate such advice to some degree. In summary, if enough data is available, DL can allow any industry to understand its customers or market much better, and therefore, automate engagements with them.

Congratulations! You have now finished this technical section. Hopefully, you have a good understanding of how different AI techniques work and what you can use them for. Time for us to get ready to learn why so many efforts in adopting AI today tend to fail and what it will take you to succeed with AI solutions, responsibly.

Conclusion

Deep learning is useful because of the immense volume of data it can analyze accurately, even if not always in the quickest manner. It has been made possible because our need to quickly and accurately analyze exponentially increasing volumes of data has matched with the increase in computing power to be able to process all that information. Storing that information has historically been tough but progressive. We are quickly arriving at the ability to store vast amounts of data in DNA. That said, the processing capability of deep learning also serves as a limitation due to its dependence on large amounts of data.

Deep learning allows AI to evolve from an intelligent machine that can make predictions, reveal insights, communicate, and learn from its mistakes, to start thinking like humans. ANN makes this possible by analyzing and computing numerous combinations of variables with different weights to provide an output. It is the same approach, followed by neurons in the human brain. ANN also allows a cost check to go back and revise the weights to minimize the errors in the outputs.

Processing images, however, requires translating them into a list of variables to serve as inputs. That is where CNN comes in. CNN extracts the key features of images and processes it in steps to render a collection of input variables that can be fed just the way inputs were fed in nodes into ANN.

Questions

1. Is this statement true or false? The sheer volume of data reception and exchange deep learning can handle, and the rigor of this technique means that if there is a deep learning solution available to solve our business problem, we should go for it.

2. Deep Learning may not work if an organization does not have enough ....

3. Which of the following factors have made deep learning possible and attractive:

   I. The exponentially growing volume of data

   II. The ability to store large amounts of data in a small space

   III. The ability to process large amounts of data quickly & cheaply

   IV. Our reduced ability to focus and manually compute such large amounts of data quickly

   V. The constant requirement to get richer insights

   A. I, II & III

   B. III, IV & V

    C. I, II, III & V

    D. All of the above

4. Factors that determine the problem-solving quality of deep learning are:

    I. The number of variables/input nodes

    II. The number of hidden neuron layers

    III. The activation function applied

    IV. The rigor of cost function applied

    V. The volume and correctness of data available to analyze

    VI. The time allowed for Deep Learning to improve

    A. I & II

    B. III & IV

    C. I, II, III & IV

    D. All of the above

5. Determine the right order for the following steps:

    I. Apply Activation Function to compute & generate outputs

    II. Max Pooling

    III. Feature Detection

    IV. Apply Cost Function to detect errors

    V. Flattening

    A. I > IV > III > II > V

    B. I > III > II > V > IV

    C. III > II > I > V > IV

    D. III > II > V > I > IV

Answers

1. False

Explanation: Deep learning can be costly and also requires significantly large volumes of data, which businesses may not ordinarily have. It is why most businesses stick with machine learning.

2. Data
3. D
4. D
5. D

Section - III
Using AI Successfully and Responsibly

Welcome to Section 3 of the AI journey. Having looked at how to prepare for and start an AI journey to solve a business problem, and which techniques or solutions may prove useful, we will now learn how to go about the process required to deploy and use an AI software in the right way, and to avoid failures of investments that most organizations, unfortunately, have to deal with today. We will also spare a moment to understand how the value of AI can be very different from what we may estimate. The last chapter will look at how to use AI ethically and responsibly through careful strategic planning and policy formulation. And why it is necessary to mitigate the risks posed by AI. You will learn:

- How to measure AI's performance
- How to get others to use it in the organization
- How to implement it successfully so that you don't waste thousands of dollars and hours of effort
- How to estimate the financial value of an AI solution
- How to formulate AI strategies (Best practices)
- How to frame a sound AI policy (7 principles of Human-AI Work Policy)
- How to minimize the risks associated with AI

The chapters included are:

- **Chapter 9: AI Adoption and Valuation**
- **Chapter 10: AI Strategy, Policy and Risk Management**

By the end, you will have finally arrived at the very forefront of AI knowledge and its associated dilemmas and questions today. The book will close with an epilogue contrasting a promising future vs. a dystopian one, and how our response to AI's challenges can determine the future it creates.

CHAPTER 9
AI Adoption and Valuation

By now, you have learned how to decide whether to use AI, become data ready, and choose the right AI solution. Now we come to its deployment in the organization. People and process have to go hand-in-hand for good performance, as processes are built around, and designed to enable, people. The success of AI adoption depends on its effective use and the business impact it has, both of which have to be measured. For the robot to improve in accuracy and its choice of drink, Maya ideally has to use the robot regularly and properly. That may involve feed in the correct data and updating the AI model as needed. Proper usage of AI involves phases that any team must closely follow. Equally important is to get a sense of its value, given the investments that have been put into it.

Structure

In this chapter, we will discuss the following topics:

- Phases of the AI deployment process
- Measuring and comparing AI's benefits and costs (AI scenario analysis)

- Issues facing the employee adoption of AI
- AI valuation approach

Objective

After studying this chapter, you should be able to:

- Better make a case for choosing an AI or a non-AI solution to solve a problem
- Put the right metrics in place
- Get buy-ins from stakeholders in AI use
- Get users trained in an adaptable and persuasive phased manner
- Estimate the valuation of an AI software asset or firm
- Understand why AI software valuations differ from traditional software

9.1 Phases of AI deployment

There are three phases in AI deployment: pre-deployment, deployment, and post-deployment. During these three phases, organizations have to deal with two major risks: justifying the decision to use a particular AI solution to the leadership and stakeholders and getting buy-ins from employees to use it well. The former becomes the focus in Phase 1 and while the latter takes center-stage in Phases 2 and 3.

9.1.1 Phase 1 – Pre-deployment

Let's start with phase 1, which is before deployment. Tracking the employee adoption rate and quantifying the business impact of results from AI is important to keep in touch with whether the model is working properly. Remember that as AI learns with new incoming information, it may become more accurate or even more biased. We have to be able to know when either happens. The metrics chosen by a manager to review performance have to be set in phase 1 itself for two reasons: First, the measures that you will put in place beforehand will allow employees to get trained on them in a more planned manner. Second, the measures have to indicate early whether the chosen AI solution that you have decided to go with is likely to be the best option to solve a problem.

The measures that we focus on also depend on the choice of the software and whether we are building or buying it. For instance, building software in-house may require us to consider the cost and quality of development and testing, which may not be needed otherwise. Likewise, AI software may surface variables in a company's operation that are key to predicting costs, which we would otherwise not have looked at. It is why the metrics are finalized in a phased manner.

So how do you choose the right metrics? One option is to follow a stepwise **AI Scenario Analysis** that compares the benefits and costs of alternative scenarios. Here is the approach:

1. **Identify scenarios:** There are generally five scenarios in play:
   - Buy an AI solution
   - Build an AI solution
   - Buy a non-AI solution
   - Build a non-AI solution
   - Do nothing

   The fifth option is the current state and serves as our' control' or default to compare against. It could be that some of the other options are out of the question for an organization. For example, most organizations may be in a position to build an AI solution so that that piece can be left out. We should pen down only the ones that are realistically under consideration.

2. **Benefits comparison:** We now compare the benefits served by the scenarios about the control/default scenario. Generally, any AI tool has one or more of five broad benefits:
   - It makes solving a problem possibly
   - It makes solving a problem easier
   - It makes solving a problem cheaper
   - It makes solving a problem quicker
   - It provides a better solution altogether, for instance, making more accurate predictions

   Not all of these benefits may apply to each scenario, nor may they be served equally. Looking at the benefits—with regards to their importance to the organization and their impact level, in comparison to the option of *doing nothing* can help shortlist the scenarios further, ideally to two scenarios. These comparisons can be subjective or numerical at this stage, depending on the comfort of the manager. Remember that we are not yet looking at KPI's, but only dealing with estimates at this point.

3. **Cost comparison:** For the final two, we look at the costs, which are primarily incurred in three areas:

   - **Financial:** This includes the money spent on purchasing or building software, in getting it deployed and used, and other hidden costs. It also includes market loss due to competitive disadvantage, or opportunity/sunk costs that increase as more time is spent on AI journeys that go on and on for an extended time.

   - **Personnel:** From changes in employee performance to those in their motivation levels to even low engagements can all add to unforeseen costs.

   - **Process:** Given the time and process involved in deploying software, incorporating its insights, an AI journey can hinder existing processes in an organization, including the ones that were created for other software previously, thereby resulting in collateral losses and disruptive change in the organization.

   Once again, the criticality of each cost area and the impact level in each shortlisted scenario can be compared to the option of doing nothing to justify the prevailing best option, if there is indeed one. The approach followed can again be subjective or numerical.

4. **Set KPIs:** So far, we have worked with estimates of the importance and impact levels in each scenario. Now, we come to set up **key performance indicators (KPIs)** to measure the actuals for the chosen alternative in comparison to the current state of doing nothing different. Since the metrics relate to the option under consideration, this step will allow you to identify specific indicators that you will be tracking as the solution deployment goes ahead. The KPI's correspond to each benefit and cost area that has been considered. There is no finite number on how many KPIs you can use, but it is always better to have a few and critical ones. If required, you can use a cascading technique, with high-level KPIs in each area set in the first level, broken down into more detailed ones in the second level, and so on.

This process can help you with an initial justification for your choice and keep you on track with the AI tools' performance and its value to the business:

GOAL: CHOOSE THE RIGHT METRICS

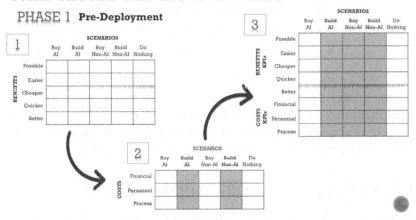

Figure 9.1: *Benefit-cost analysis template*

As time goes by, once an AI solution has been agreed to, developed, and is ready to deploy, it's time to start preparing for AI adoption by the employees in the company. It is key to note that a **Champion** and **Super Users** have to be inducted in Phase 1 for buy-in ideally. Their roles, however, become prominent in Phases 2 and 3 as we discuss next.

9.1.2 Phase 2 – Deployment

Let's move on to phase 2, which comes during deployment. The primary roadblocks organizations face with getting their employees to buy-in is that:

- Employees face confusion due to an overly large and complex technological stack that's already existing in the company. Stack fatigue is a very real thing.

- Entering data for AI to work takes a lot of employees' time that hinders their work.

- Insights or recommendations provided by AI sometimes go against what the employee would prefer or can even make their work less useful, thereby creating a conflict.

Communication here is key as employees have to be clearly explained a few things in phase 2:

- Why is AI being used to solve a problem?
- What it can and cannot do?
- What does it need from employees to function properly?
- How can employees and the organization benefit from it?
- How does it not pose a risk to employee performance and job security?

Process-wise, the second phase is also where the most successful organizations I've seen normally have a Champion overseeing this entire journey. The Champion oversees the deployment and acts as a bridge between senior management and other employees.

9.1.3 Phase 3 – Post-deployment

It brings us to phase 3, which is after deployment. Once AI is deployed, the Champion first trains select employees in the organization called Super Users who can role-model the use of AI with other employees in their teams. Super Users are the early adopters in the organization and are responsible for getting buy-ins from and train all the other users in their teams. User training generally focuses on helping users learn:

- How to use the solution correctly to get the most value
- How to apply the solution results to daily work objectives
- When to use the solution
- How to feed incorrect data in a regular manner
- How the solutions and the employee's performance will be measured

We have now looked at the trio of people, processes, and performance measurements that form the pillars of successful AI usage. But even if the right solution is found, appropriate data is available, and people and processes are in place to back it up. AI journey can meet a premature end simply because it failed to meet incoherent or unrealistic expectations, or because the conditions changed. Perhaps the biggest challenge of them all is to see what may be invisible. Bias and lack of fairness. It can be tricky, and in many cases, an organization can go on trusting insights from AI without realizing that it is inaccurate in certain situations. It is something that has already been happening with so many research studies that come out—new ones that become the accepted gospel until some other study comes out and somewhat discards the earlier finding. Consider, for instance, the robot serving Maya tea without realizing that she may also want a cookie with it on some days, simply because Maya chooses to get the cookie herself rather than asking the robot for it.

Despite an early validation of the solution and successful adoption, it takes sustained process thinking to keep generating value from AI. It also requires a clear understanding of the asset value to get continued support from the leadership. It is where AI solutions depart from typical software not only in their continued usage but also in how they are valued. So how do we sustain the value of AI and determine its true valuation?

9.2 AI Investment and Valuation

Any investment requires some clarity of the value one can expect out of it, whether for an investor or a company developing its own AI solution. The following **AI Valuation Approach** can help make this estimation by looking at three factors, assuming a stable economy. These are:

1. Nature of the offering (for example, pure software versus software and service mix)
2. Business scalability
3. The phase of technology evolution

9.2.1 Nature of the offering

AI can be delivered as hardware, software, or service. The confusion generally occurs because the boundaries between the three are not distinct. For instance, it is not inaccurate to consider an AI solution as another software, but one would certainly be mistaken in necessarily treating the business model as such.

Traditional software has a distinct advantage in its scalability and the margins it brings home once ready. The installation cost aside; the software can continue to offer its benefits without significant ongoing efforts from the vendor. As such, software companies have often been valued at up to 8-10x the revenue. On the other hand, services like consulting are valued differently because one usually has to create value from scratch with every client or project. Their valuation has been as low as 1-2x the revenue. AI can be very different, particularly in the B2B space.

While B2C solutions can be simple plug-and-play software, a B2B AI business model is usually a software-and-service model, whether packed in hardware or not. While the core solution may be software, it is one that requires a significant service component, whether internally or for a client. There are three phases of service involved:

1. The first service requirement comes in framing the problem, data pre-processing and training the AI model.

2. The second service requirement belongs to the customization and retraining of the model, in sync with the client's business realities and needs, as well as the training of the end-users.

   Once a model is rendered, AI has had its say and has generated an output. However, even the pre-processed data may be carrying a lot of assumptions about the business that are not true or no longer relevant. It is usually the part where the business side and the technical side sit together to review the results and the underlying factors that AI has considered, to validate or tweak them, another case for why explainability in AI helps.

   Once the business side is satisfied with the working model, users must be trained to help them catch up on how to get the most from the solution and to ensure it keeps working that way.

3. The third service requirement is an ongoing, periodic check and retraining of the model every time the conditions change.

This phase, in particular, is where AI departs the most from traditional software. Even with a working model, the accuracy of insights may drop over time with changes in data or the business model. Unforeseen biases may surface, or the technology may evolve. The objectives of the business may change, thereby rendering a new version of the problem statement. Even the insights coming in from AI may prompt the business to take corrective action or change their way of doing things. Any of these situations can subject the model to a new reality that it has not learned well enough to understand yet. A natural learning curve can take time for machine learning, depending on the volume and frequency of new data coming in. It is why AI requires continued focus from not just the customer success manager but the data scientists as well.

The effort and time involves is why similar revenues generated by a pure software vs. a software & service model, garner different valuation. Mathematically, a software and service model could put an AI valuation at 4-5x the revenues it generates.

9.2.2 Business scalability

Mathematics aside, the customization an AI solution often required for every new customer also limit its scalability and therefore, impacts valuation. Valuation at face value of the current revenue size & velocity in an AI software is one side of the coin. An AI company's valuation can also get points for the market it operates in, the growth in revenue it generates, the discounted cash flow, the skill it brings in its team, and the more intangible assets such as the database developed and the barriers to entry created. In the end, few basic metrics always hold true:

- First is the ease of integration and level of customization needed with every new client for an AI solution. (1). It is also why solutions that focus on a few clear use cases generally perform better.

- Second is a more traditional focus on the business efficiency to repay any additional dollar spent on sales and marketing, and its predictability in terms of sustainable customer growth and retention. (2).

Low retention rates may not always be due to AI. It can often be due to over-expectation on the part of the customer or the organizational leadership. That is what makes the job of the marketers, the sales account executives, and the customer success manager so important in AI, to set and manage expectations and to educate the customer, or the internal leadership, on this technology from the outset.

Valuation in the technology domain is generally also determined by comparable exits that other similar companies have seen. However, this is tricky in the case of AI because the market has seen some exaggerated investments, with many riding on hype and lack of understanding of AI among many investors. As per a 2019 report, AI startups made approximately $5 billion worth of equity deals in 2016, and this value was growing by approximately 50% every year. (3). The valuation was expected to normalize as investors become more informed and experienced on AI. Let us now look at how these phases influence an AI firm's value.

9.2.3 The phase of technology evolution

The valuations for pure software and a mix of software and services can vary at different stages of technological evolution. Assuming these two as the maximum and minimum limits, respectively, AI's valuation within this range is likely to follow the specific technology's hype cycle, as per the curve originally developed by Gartner. Accordingly, any new technology goes through five stages at varying speeds, which include a peak point of inflated expectations, followed by a low trough of disillusionment before the expectation and reality match and stabilize. Not all AI techniques are at the same stage. For example, NLP, machine learning, and deep learning were all spread out between the peak and trough stages as of 2019. (4).

Based on observation, I assume that an AI firm's valuation, which is driven by both hype and actual performance, closely follows this curve within the two extremes of pure software valuation and software and services valuation. However, the specific reach of an AI company's valuation curve would be further defined by the extent of the services component involves in its offering.

As an example, for two AI firms with similar revenues, but one with a pure software model and one with a mix of software and service, the resultant drift in those AI firms' valuations between the two extremes could look something like the dotted lines in the figure below. Note, however, that the dotted line trends are purely an estimate, drawn for ease of understanding:

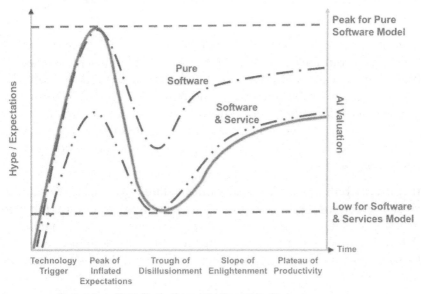

Figure 9.2: AI valuation estimates

So, an AI company's valuation may follow either of the dotted curves, or something in between—depending on the extent of services involved with every customer. On that particular trend line, the company could be further ahead or behind across the five stages, depending on its specific technology and its evolution. Then again, at that specific point, the valuation may further vary due to the business' scalability. As we can see, there are quite a few variables that can impact how a solution or company is valued at any point of time.

We have so far focused on sustaining an AI journey and its value, which is one side of the coin. The other side deals with its sustainable development and value in a social sense. While AI needs investment from both private investors and government, they are not always in sync with each other. For instance, while private companies have the funds to invest in AI research, they are often more interested in specific studies that benefit them. Without the companies' active involvement, the research centers may not always be in touch with the end-users of the study and can remain oblivious to the practical challenge's companies are facing and would likely require AI for. Moreover, business executives generally do not fully understand

AI themselves yet to drive the research direction or the investment decision in this space.

Among the issues above, conflict of interest is one to take particular note of as a company can easily be more likely to invest in AI research that gives it a distinct advantage, and may not publicly share the findings to preserve competitive foothold. The AI it develops may also not necessarily be fair or ethically sound. That robs the industry from making progress collectively and responsibly. A case in point would be the fact that lobbyists are gaining an understanding of AI faster than lawmakers. (5).

It presents both an ethical and policy-related question. We require clear governance policies for AI in an organization to manage its risks – both apparent and hidden. That may single-handedly determine if we create AI that empowers us or one that eventually turns into something more destructive. That will be the last topic of our discussion.

Conclusion

Even a good AI solution needs a careful deployment process to be practically effective. These include pre-deployment, deployment, and post-deployment stages. The first stage requires us to put in place provisional measures on the benefits and costs associated with choosing a particular AI solution over other options. These estimations can help us justify our decision. The deployment phase is where an AI Champion is put in place to be the link between the business and technical teams. The Champion also begins to position select Super Users and get them on board on why AI is being used, what it can or cannot do, what it needs from them, how the company can benefit from it, and what the risks are to the Super Users and their teams. These early adopters help improve the AI solution by exposing issues in its usage. Once AI is deployed, we enter the post-deployment phase, where Super Users carry the knowledge to inform, advise, and train other users in their respective teams. A critical element of this learning is also to cover what the users need to do to keep getting the most out of the AI software.

The financial value of AI software is often different from that of traditional software. While it is tricky to standardize this, AI's valuation may be 4-5x the revenue as per traditional valuation methods, which is lower and not higher than that of traditional software. It is because AI involves an inevitable service component that accompanies the software, particularly in B2B. It includes customizing AI models, retraining it periodically, and training the users. That said, AI companies often see their valuation skyrocket, primarily due to the promise of what it can do and be worth in the long run. We need to balance both these extremes by paying attention to the specific use case, AI's capability, collateral impact, and the changing conditions that will inform the AI model.

Questions

1. AI generally has which of the following benefits:

   I. It makes solving a problem possibly.

   II. It makes solving a problem easier.

   III. It makes solving a problem cheaper.

   IV. It makes solving a problem quicker.

   V. It provides a better solution altogether, for instance, making more accurate predictions.

   A. None of the above

   B. I, III & V

   C. II & IV

   D. All of the above

2. Which of the following are true about successful AI adoption by internal or external stakeholders:

   I. People need clarity on why AI is being used and how it will affect/help them

   II. People usually need proper training on how to use AI well

   III. People need a champion they identify with to lead the AI initiative

   IV. The champion can work alone in driving AI adoption in the team

   V. It is sufficient to measure the accuracy and bottom-line impact of results from the AI software to determine if it was successful

    A. I, II & III

    B. IV & V

    C. I, II, III & V

    D. All of them

3. An accurate estimation of the financial value of an AI solution is needed to sustain support from the investors and / or company leadership. An AI business model is usually a combination of .... and ...., and should be valued accordingly.

4. Is this statement true or false? AI solutions generally require services in the form of training and retraining the model, and training the users. But if nothing in the customer's business or data changes, the AI model will likely not require further checks.

5. Is this statement true or false? Ease of integration of an AI solution in a customer's tech stack and the level of customization needed for that customer are crucial metrics in determining the valuation and growth potential of the AI company.

Answers

1. D

2. A

   Explanation: A Champion needs support, including superusers, to drive adoption. Meanwhile, the success of AI also depends on its associated and hidden costs as well as adoption levels and collateral impact on other processes in the organization.

3. Software, Service

4. False

   Explanation: In theory, if there are no changes to the business or data, an AI model does not require retraining. However, in practice, tangible or intangible changes are common and almost always in play. The way AI is being used by every user in the organization also makes a difference. Such unknowns necessitate periodic checks even if only to ensure that the model is behaving properly.

5. True

CHAPTER 10
AI Strategy, Policy and Risk Management

Welcome to the final lesson. We have so far seen what an AI Journey in an organization typically involves. I saved the first step of that journey for the end because it is the most important one throwing all the questions back at us. The answers need to come from the organizational leadership but require dialogue among all stakeholders. We are talking about strategic policy and risk management.

Structure

In this chapter, we will discuss the following topics:
- Best practices of AI strategy formulation
- Seven principles of Human-AI work policy
- AI ethics & challenges
- Systems and socioeconomic risk
- Privacy and security risk
- Legal and financial risk

Objective

After studying this chapter, you should be able to:

- Appreciate the need for a robust and thorough policy and strategy around AI development and use
- Formulate effective strategies around AI
- Frame a sound AI policy
- Learn the major risk areas related to AI
- Understand which jobs can be replaced by AI and which ones can't
- Understand the importance of explainable AI vs. Blackbox AI
- Realize the dilemmas and challenges facing us today in the field of AI

10.1 Strategy formulation

An AI journey requires an investment of time and money, training of both the AI model and its end users, and policies to govern its performance effectively and ethically. All of these tie into the organizational strategy. There are a few best practices that can help weave a clear strategy around AI. These include:

- Start small, with a low-risk pilot
- Gauge the level of support and expectations from the leadership
- Be clear on why a team wants to use AI before undertaking a project
- Involve managers from all relevant teams to gauge project feasibility
- Identify the roles, responsibilities, and accountabilities

Let us delve further into these points. **It is generally recommended to start with a small, low-risk AI pilot.** Making an AI project too big and complex, with too many players involved, often leads to failure. It can be due to unforeseen complications, requirements surpassing estimations, or lack of collaboration among stakeholders, among other reasons. That said, no matter how small the AI project, **it needs support from the leadership and is often defined by the extent and nature of that support.** As sponsors, leaders must understand the investment and risks involved, and be clear in their expectations of the result. Without appropriate leadership approval, AI projects will either be shelved midway, occur in the disorganized, disparate manner in different departments, or prove unsuccessful because few or all of the other requirements of a successful AI journey that we saw earlier were not met – from data to employee readiness.

Strategy formulation also requires thorough thinking on why a team wants to use AI. Is it to gain a competitive advantage or to keep up with the times? Is it to solve a pressing problem in a better way with better results or lower costs or for some other reason? Any strategy needs to be working towards a clear vision if you want to avoid a messy situation later, where teams could find themselves stuck midway with below-par results.

Suppose Maya went and bought a brand-new all-in-one house robot from a local store. She needs her post-work beverage, and a similar robot has been doing that successfully for a friend of hers. Consider the things that could go wrong. She may initially learn that she can simply instruct the robot to get her a particular drink, which is great. However, the robot does not accurately understand her accent. So, Maya now purchases an Alexa or Google Home-type gear to the plugin for better communication so that the robot can understand what Maya means. However, she soon finds that the robot cannot bend too low or rise too high, nor navigate the intermittent stairs in Maya's house, to reach the shelves where the cutlery is kept. Finally, the effort and costs involved to train and operate the robot properly may end up being so high that Maya, for all practical purposes, comes to rarely use it over the long term. It is the story with so many gadgets we purchase in our day-to-day lives. AI is no different.

The fit of an AI software in the organization is often dependent on each respective team that will enable, manage, or uses it. Therefore, **the strategy formulation should also involve managers from all relevant teams to gauge feasibility.** Once understood, it allows the teams to set up an indication of the time, the budget and the effort that they're required to spend, and allows you to get everyone's commitment to the cause.

Multi-stakeholder involvement leaves us with a pressing question: Who should be accountable for the different aspects of an AI journey? Moreover, if an AI software results in business loss, which is to blame: the end-users, the project manager, the data scientists, the senior leadership, or the vendor? **An AI strategy helps informs the RACI framework** we discussed earlier, to identify who is responsible, accountable, to be consulted, and kept informed to ensure its effective execution and crisis management.

10.2 7 Principles of Human-AI Work Policy

An appreciation of an organization's broad strategic interests and objectives facilitates seamless AI policy framing and is also guided by it. Any organization needs a policy framework in place to guide the use of AI and to guard itself against malpractices, either in third-party solutions it adopts or in the behavior of its employees. A sound policy helps inform the way AI is developed, deployed, and used. As a good frame of reference, you can find Google's stand on responsible AI on its webpage titled *Responsible AI Practices. (1)*.

Policy framing involves a few key points that chiefly relate to how AI and humans are to work together. We have discussed these components at different stages throughout this book. To bring them all together, it is best to see them from the perspective of the end user's relationship with AI. We had previously looked at the seven principles of an AI journey. Let us now look at the seven principles of human-AI work relationship that can guide an organization's AI policy framing. Each of the points that we discuss next can help frame the corresponding guideline in a policy document:

1. **AI as a Child:** Like with any child, an AI tool has to be properly trained, and it's learning and development over time has to be monitored. That takes effort and patience. The policy must emphasize the need for timing considerations and setting the right measures in any AI project undertaken in the company.

2. **AI as a Friend:** AI can be exciting. But the arrival of a new friend doesn't mean that you forget the old friends (in this case, old tools that have served you well). An organization should always mandate an objective justification of bringing in a new AI tool, and an assessment of its collateral impact on existing systems and processes.

3. **AI as a Pet:** You may be enamored with it, but it has to be accepted by all in the house (read: the team). It can't be adopted by some and ignored or mistreated by others. Employee acceptance and proper adoption of AI should be a priority for companies to avoid the failure of investments.

4. **AI as a Colleague:** You and AI are a team. The tool has been built and tasked to do specific things; so, don't expect it to do everything for you. It needs you just as you need it. The policy document is a great opportunity for companies also to reiterate the importance of current employees, and to position AI as a tool – not a magic wand – designed to support them.

5. **AI as a Grandparent:** AI may have a lot of wise insights, but they are almost entirely based on past data, which may or may not be valid in every future situation. Listen to AI but understand the context and background, so that you can make effective decisions. No business decision should be blindly based on AI insights, and organizations have to make that stand clear.

6. **AI as a Partner:** Whether we imagine this partnership as business or personal, it's one that cannot easily be brought in and thrown away. It's important to do a thorough check and be sure not to jump too soon or too late. Good timing and mutual fit are crucial. The policy document should allow any AI project to be undertaken only when the organization (or team) is AI-ready. It should also enable proactiveness in AI enablement to avoid delays and lagging behavior that could result in a competitive disadvantage.

7. **AI as a Being:** There have been talks of AI's ethical needs. In 2017, Sophia even became the world's first robot to be granted citizenship. (2) The point is that you should treat AI (or any tool) as a being. It means acknowledging that it has to be fed well (the food being good data), and more importantly, that it should not be misused. It can allow policies to inform procedures to sustain responsible use and positive results from AI.

That final point on misuse of AI is critical in several ways, each concerned with the various risks that AI brings with it. These risks can lend additional points in the policy document to ensure they are managed well. The next section looks at what these risks are and the challenges or questions facing us today as a result.

10.3 Risks with AI

Without a proper policy in place, organizations are subject to three broad areas of risk. While not a comprehensive list, these include:

- Systems and socioeconomic risk
- Privacy and security risk
- Legal and financial risk

The point to note here is this: Each of these risks come with associated dilemmas facing us today. The right approach to managing them often boils down to what the right balance of ethics and practicality is for you. As we will see, that balance itself tends to shift when we have personal stakes in play.

10.3.1 Systems and socioeconomic risk

Let's start with the systems and socioeconomic risk. It primarily pertains to the risk of replacing existing systems and resources. Any new technological innovation that transforms a socioeconomic cycle results in the extinction of processes and jobs that served older technologies and systems, which are replaced by newer processes and jobs based on the requirements to support the new system.

A complete overhaul in an organization is rarely advisable, regardless of how often we may feel tempted to do so. Consider the example of an AI investment agent that performed better than three portfolio managers in a 2012 study. That performance could easily be mistaken for the AI's superiority in investment-related decision making. Yet, the AI was likely not capable of understanding the sudden jumps or crashes in the stock market or catching the subtle reactions of management to questions in an investor meeting—from the twitch of an eye to a nervous hesitation, that investors can use to detect if the management is hiding something. (3).

Managers must protect themselves from the fallacy of committing to a new shiny object by disregarding what they already have. In fact, in almost every consulting project around AI enablement and use that I have been part of, we have had to start with the basics to get the data dictionary in place for the client: with traditional processes, data sources, owners and workflows having to be properly mapped out. Any new AI solution is then designed to utilize what is in place while causing minimal intrusion as far as feasible.

Coming to the risk to resources: Like any new technological insurgent in an economy over the centuries, the risk posed by AI on our socioeconomic structure is about a balance between the jobs it eliminates and the ones it creates, and about the general levels of wellbeing it offers us. Think about the typists who moved to a different skill once typewriters were replaced by computers. Or the case of Vancouver's dairy farmer, Diana West, who employed robots that could milk cows and even tell when a cow was having an infection or when she was in heat. At her farm, the workers simply moved from managing the cows to managing the robots. (4) The question is: Is it always a 1:1 ratio between the jobs lost and ones created? Consider a different dairy farmer – in New Hampshire in the US. In this case, the robot had given hope to the farmer's struggling farm business by helping improve efficiency and cut costs; only, it had done so by making up for four full-time employees! (5). If you're wondering what the extent of risk of jobs being replaced by AI is, think about the first step we learned in undertaking an AI journey: problem framing. If you'd recall, any problem had to be broken down into individual tasks or use cases that AI may solve. Likewise, it is the tasks within a job that AI replaces. The overall impact on any job, therefore, depends on the number of tasks handled by that job that AI can reliably replace.

If you'd like to gauge the impact of AI on jobs in your organization, here's a thumb rule to follow: Any task that is rule-based is potentially replaceable by AI as it matures. These are tasks that are performed as per set rules and procedures in a largely predictable and unchanging set of scenarios. On the other hand, more interpersonal tasks, operate in unpredictable scenarios or involve critical decision making that may not abide by strict rules will require humans for the foreseeable future. For example, a pilot flying a plane based on strict rules as per the rulebook and guided by tower stations may be replaced by a robot. However, you'd still need a human in the cockpit for critical decision making in emergencies. An air hostess, meanwhile, may have an automated trolley stroll through the aisle and serve food to the passengers but may have to deal with passenger queries and in-flight conduct herself.

The dilemma facing us is this: to an extent, employing AI allows organizations to cut costs and sustain themselves financially so that they and all other jobs can survive. It also allows organizations to remove any inherent discrimination and inefficiencies that humans may bring. Robots are also loyal. Yet, all that could come at the cost of a loss of livelihood for someone whose job was replaced, even if that person wasn't as efficient or loyal. Moreover, the overuse of AI can also blind a company to biases in the AI model's decision making and, of course, rob it of the power to make intuitive or critical contextual decisions, costing it dearly. So how should you or an organization decide when and to what degree it is okay to employ AI to perform tasks?

10.3.2 Privacy and security risk

In its thirst for data, AI can easily and illegally breach into customers' and users' private information. It can also use approaches or make predictions that are either unethical or biased.

Suppose Maya's robot was linked to her cell phone and found that a disagreement with her boss or colleagues at work strongly affect her choice of drink in the evening when she comes back home. In its quest to become more and more accurate in predicting what Maya will drink, the robot may start to analyze Maya's daily behavior, search and browsing history on her phone, and so on. If uncontrolled and, if possible, it may even try to tap into information about her colleagues. There'd be no end to it. So how do we teach AI right and wrong?

A curious example would be that of Microsoft's Tay AI; a chatbot launched briefly in 2016 to interact with real people on social media. Unfortunately, people on social media started feeding it racist and anti-feminist inputs. Soon enough, Tay became racist and anti-feminist. Consider Google's case, on the other hand. Following the criticism around its collaboration around military drones with the U.S. Department of Defense, it launched a board of experts to guide the responsible development and use of AI. The board had to be disbanded shortly after as some of the members turned out to be openly in support of drones or were anti-LGBTQ, anti-trans, and anti-immigrant. (6).

What we are talking about here is as much a systems risk as a security risk because a biased AI system can easily act unfairly against those it is biased against—whether it is one individual or a whole community. Think about a tool tested by the American Civil Liberties Union in 2018 that incorrectly identified 28 members of Congress as having been arrested for a crime, disproportionately picking out African American lawmakers, including civil rights icon John Lewis! Then again, in contrast, AI is also what allowed New Delhi police to use image recognition to examine a database of 45,000 kids living in shelters and homes, which helped the police trace 2,930 missing children in four days! (7).

We are a species with individually varying standards of morality, ethics, rights, and wrongs. On a broader scale, the majority of us can agree to those definitions in many situations. That may be a good place to start, but invariably, we will arrive at points of dilemma and conflict. So how do we teach AI a constant standard to adhere to? Or shall we look to AI to eventually guide us around certain foundational standards? Here's how IBM is tackling bias in AI: **https://www.youtube.com/watch?v=q44XUZdCIMM**.

A person has the right to own and control the use of data related to him or her. One can argue that he or she should also have the right to be forgotten in terms of their digital footprint. But while that can ensure privacy for an individual, what happens if we lose all or relevant information related to someone who then goes on to commit a crime or is unknowingly carrying a transmissible disease?

One can surmise that it may be helpful to keep at least basic personal information out of the domain of privacy. Yet, that thought gets quickly put into question when one thinks of Samsung's Deepfake that can generate an entire video from a single profile pic, as it did from a single portrait of the Mona Lisa! (8). So, if your Facebook profile pic is mandatorily publicly visible, an entirely fake video of a real-looking you are talking and expressing, may not be far away if the technology were to fall into the wrong hands.

You may be wondering why a company would generate software this risky. The intention is not necessarily evil, as sometimes, the very nature of AI development to solve a problem teeters on the edge of risk. A good example would be Grover, created by the University of Washington and Allen Institute for AI, that can write fake news articles! The intention behind it is to understand better the properties of fake information to detect one. (9). Fake news is a big problem, after all. What we must guard against is the misuse of such technology not only by external sources but also by the employees within that can compromise an organization's security. That brings us to the third risk area.

10.3.3 Legal and financial risk

Legal and financial risk has largely to do with repercussions of AI misuse - intentionally or unintentionally, particularly with black-box AI.

With sound policies in place, it is important that you, as any other user, always opt for transparent AI solutions and not black boxes. We have already discussed this a few times. Ethical AI, responsible AI, transparent AI, explainable AI, xAI, trusted AI—these are all different terms used to address the same issue. Such solutions, unlike traditional AI, are built to reveal the rationale behind the insights they are providing so that the users can understand and get the context to obey or ignore those insights.

Generally speaking, the more automated and self-learning AI becomes, the less visibility we have into how it is analyzing something. Consider Deep Learning, which looks at many, many factors. It is naturally difficult to reveal all those factors and the corresponding conditions involved in its decision-making. And that brings us to the final ethical dilemma we are faced with today: How to balance explainability and robustness of AI insights if they are often inversely correlated? The answer is contextual.

AI can afford to be a black box if it is dealing with a relatively simple task in that particular context. An example would be correctly identifying the picture of a dog. However, AI needs to explain its rationale when it deals with more critical tasks like filtering resumes in recruiting. After all, while AI can identify the presence of skills or look for success indicators in the wording on a resume, it cannot beat the depth of assessment we can make by physically interacting with the candidates and looking at their body language. Plus, recruiters make a good deal of decisions on intuition, which is not necessarily explainable.

On the other hand, if AI were not involved at all, recruiters would have a tough time going through hundreds of resumes for a job. They would likely make an even narrower or an even more biased assessment than the AI would have, in terms of that initial filtering. It is a perfect example of why the best and most secure business solutions today are derived by people and AI working together.

AI's job is to enhance the productivity of humans. It can show us things we couldn't see otherwise and make a lot of our tasks easier and quicker. But it cannot be the sole decision-maker. The final decision should always rest with humans if an organization wishes to avoid falling into legal trouble or suffer unforeseen financial losses, besides going ethically astray. Some degree of explainability in AI's analysis is important for humans to be able to see and interpret what AI is saying and why it is saying whatever it's saying, to make informed and contextual decisions. It is why human intervention will always remain important in my view.

What about cases where health is involved, or something more personal? In the US, the FDA recently announced that it is developing a framework for regulating self-learning AI products in medicine. (10). But consider the AI solution that can detect cancer more accurately than doctors can. It does a great job in early detection but lacks the subtle, judgment making skills that doctors have in diagnosing patients. For instance, it cannot distinguish cancers that can kill people from ones that may be a false positive case of not at all dangerous even in the long term (although, to be fair, doctors can also make false-positive assessments). After all, a highly accurate AI is trained to spot even small lesions to detect cancer, potentially resulting in over-diagnosis, since there are no gold standards for what constitutes cancer. (11). Moreover, doctors may not always know how AI solutions come to their conclusions. So, if you were identified by AI as potentially at risk of cancer, should the doctors trust the AI blindly to start treating you before it is even confirmed that your case is not false and is expected to be life-threatening? Or should they avoid blind trust and wait until those symptoms start to show more explicitly so that the doctors can manually detect and confirm the risk of your disease?

Conclusion

This chapter dealt with a topic that precedes all others in an AI journey. It relates to formulating a robust strategy to guide those journeys and framing a sound policy to govern them. These are the most important tasks for organizational leadership as without these; AI can be ineffective because one or more of its requirements were not met. Projects can also be shelved midway due to a lack of expected results. An organization may even see disorganized projects across the organization with limited or inaccurate results. A clear strategy and policy help set the right expectations, get support from all stakeholders, and ensure that leaders understand the investments and risks.

Many risks come with the benefits AI provides. We can view them in three areas. First are the Systems and Socioeconomic risk, which is related primarily to the disruption to jobs and existing processes. We learned that not all jobs are at an equal risk of being replaced by AI. It largely boils down to how standardized the tasks are within a given job. The second risk area is that of privacy and security, which relates to personal data and surveillance. AI can easily be used in an uncomfortably intrusive manner, learning more about us than we may like. However, limiting that intrusion too much can also play out against us, robbing us of opportunities at a better life and society. The third is the legal and financial risk, which can directly impact even those companies that show sensitivity to matters of employment security and individual rights. These risks pertain to the day-to-day risks of inaccurate insights, misuse, and misinformation. BlackBox AI, in particular, should be avoided for key decisions. However, tools like Deep Learning are often not explainable but can lend the most comprehensive and contextual insights. So, as we can see, each risk today stands at a point of dilemma that needs our collective and informed efforts to manage.

Questions

1. Which of the following are true about successful AI adoption by internal and/or external stakeholders:

   I. AI projects, the data involved & the process and measures involved need to have some coherence and be part of a broader corporate strategy formulated by the leadership

   II. The ethics policy applicable to the organization would be sufficiently applicable for an AI project within the company as well

   III. Black box AI is necessarily unethical

   IV. Leaders in an organization need to understand AI and its requirements well to formulate a clear strategy and back initiatives properly

   V. If employees in an organization understand AI well, they will ensure successful use of AI in the organization

   A. I, II & III

   B. I, III, IV & V

   C. I, IV & V

   D. All of them

2. Is this statement true or false? Systems and socioeconomic risk, privacy and security risk, and legal and financial risks are the only three types of risk an organization can face with AI.

3. The threat of AI to a job depends on the number of tasks handled by that job that AI can reliably replace. Generally, any task that is or can be based on pre-specified .... is potentially replaceable by AI.

4. A clear corporate strategy can help an organization:

   I. Get support from the leadership for AI investment

   II. Understand the risks involved with AI,

   III. Avoid over-expectation of the result from AI

   A. All of them

   B. I & II

   C. II & III

   D. I & III

5. Without leadership approval, AI projects could be:

   I. Delayed but never shelved midway.

   II. Occur in a disorganized, disparate manner in different departments.

   III. Successful if at least a few of the other requirements of a successful AI journey are met.

   A. All of them

   B. II & III

   C. II only

   D. I & III

Answers

1. C

   Explanation: A Champion needs support, including superusers, to drive adoption. Meanwhile, the success of AI also depends on its associated and hidden costs as well as adoption levels and collateral impact on other processes in the organization.

2. False

    Explanation: Weapons automation, an organization's over-dependence on AI functioning without failure, AI systems interacting in a way we cannot understand, or losing human connectivity and the potential to leverage human networks, are few other examples of risks with AI.

3. Rules

4. A

5. C

Epilogue

With that last discussion on AI's ethical dilemma, you have arrived as an informed individual to the latest debate and unanswered questions around AI ethics and effectiveness. Hopefully, you now have a better understanding of what AI is, how it works, and how it can be used for the best results.

AI is not going to go away, just the way computers or the internet did not. As Victor Hugo famously said, "No army can stop an idea whose time has come." There is a lot of debate around what this army looks like and what this topic is, given the uncertainties of what this technology can do for us in the future. Like any powerful tool, it can be used for both right and wrong. But what that story looks like is up to us. What is needed is for all of us to get an understanding of AI so that we can join the conversation and influence decisions that governments and companies make. After all, ethical standards are often defined by those in power who can influence and govern them, which is why Pope Francis urged executives, investors, and regulators to be wary of the impact of AI.

AI can help optimize energy consumption to help climate change. It can develop effective antibiotics. It can also breach our privacy and reduce control over our own decision making, whether we realize it or not. On a more personal level, perhaps the more we use AI, the more we become dependent on it. After all, the quicker we get things done, the more we add tasks to fill in those empty seconds to gratify our engaged minds, and the busier we therefore become. But in being able to read our thoughts and communicate, in giving amputees a more active body part, in developing an entirely new way of fighting bacteria and illnesses within, and is even helping us understand the non-linear nature of our quantum reality, AI is shaping us both mentally and physically. In revealing our hidden biases and forcing us to root them out from our data and decisions, it is also helping us morally.

The future of AI is often interpreted to be dystopian—with killer robots; it's the defensive mindset we have inherited from our ancestors to keep us safe. But I find that the future of AI may be an evolved human species – one where we can process far more data in our brains and so be more consciously mindful of our world, have higher mental and physical capabilities to grow more than we otherwise could, reduce the collateral damage of our actions on others and on nature, and even reduce our dependency on destructive habits. With Blockchain, it can also create a secure chain of facts – what was said or discussed in meetings, for instance – to ensure there is a permanent record of truth and facts, as well as the individuals responsible, thereby rooting out fake news and misinterpretations of truth later. And as I had once defended in my university thesis many moons ago, AI can also help achieve universal basic income. If we can generate renewable energy in our house, and transfer it to someone else (say, to the neighborhood grocery as payment for groceries) – we will have effectively established a new monetary system where each of us is a producer and consumer of a universally available currency (renewable energy). A peer-trading version of that vision is already in play by companies like Power Ledger. All of these possibilities paint a very different picture in terms of what the future can hold. But to realize that, we must first be aware of AI and ensure its responsible use.

So, thank you for taking this first step in managing AI journeys. I hope you will help others understand the benefits and risks of AI as well, and will lead the dialogue and execution for many years to come. It brings us to the end of our little journey here. You can visit me at **TheUpadhyays.com** to find other helpful material or to connect. I wish you the very best for your future. Stay happy and stay productive.

References

Chapter 1 – AI Fundamentals

1. Christian, Jon. Sciencealert. 1 June 2019. *This Creepy AI Predicts What You Look Like Based on Your Voice.* **Source: https://www. sciencealert.com/this-ai-tries-to-guess-what-you-look-like-based-on-your-voice**

2. Hill, Kashmir. Forbes. 16 February 2012. *How Target Figured Out A Teen Girl Was Pregnant Before Her Father Did.* **Source: https://www.forbes.com/sites/kashmirhill/2012/02/16/how-target-figured-out-a-teen-girl-was-pregnant-before-her-father-did/#7363f4fb6668**

3. Piatetsky, Gregory. KDNuggets. 7 May 2014. *Did Target Really Predict a Teen's Pregnancy? The Inside Story.* **Source: https://www.kdnuggets.com/2014/05/target-predict-teen-pregnancy-inside-story.html**

4. McSpadden, Kevin. Time. 14 May 2015. *You Now Have a Shorter Attention Span Than a Goldfish.* **Source: https://time. com/3858309/attention-spans-goldfish/**

5. Pandya, Jayshree. Forbes. 5 July 2019. *A Changing Internet: The Convergence Of Blockchain, Internet Of Things, And Artificial Intelligence.* **Source: https://www.forbes.com/ sites/cognitiveworld/2019/07/05/a-changing-internet-the-convergence-of-blockchain-internet-of-things-and-artificial-intelligence/#53d1c7217c58**

6. Purdy, Mark & Daugherty, Paul. Accenture. 2017. *How AI Boosts Industry Profits and Innovation.* **Source: https://www. accenture.com/ca-en/insight-ai-industry-growth**

7. Verweij, Gerard & Rao, Anand. PWC. 2017. *Sizing the prize. What's the real value of AI for your business and how can you capitalise?* **Source: https://www.pwc.com/gx/en/issues/ analytics/assets/pwc-ai-analysis-sizing-the-prize-report. pdf**

8. Allen, Gregory C. CNN. 5 September 2017. *Putin and Musk are right: Whoever masters AI will run the world.* **Source: https:// www.cnn.com/2017/09/05/opinions/russia-weaponize-ai-opinion-allen/index.html**

9. Dutton, Tim. Medium. 28 June 2018. *An Overview of National AI Strategies.* **Source: https://medium.com/politics-ai/an-overview-of-national-ai-strategies-2a70ec6edfd**

10. Westerheide, Fabian. Forbes. 14 January 2020. *China – The First Artificial Intelligence Superpower.* **Source: https://www. forbes.com/sites/cognitiveworld/2020/01/14/china-artificial-intelligence-superpower/#622f7bd02f05**

11. Trafton, Anne. MIT News. 20 February 2020. *Artificial intelligence yields new antibiotic.* **Source: http://news. mit.edu/2020/artificial-intelligence-identifies-new-antibiotic-0220**

12. Rogati, Monica. Hackernoon. 12 June 2017. *The AI Hierarchy of Needs.* **https://hackernoon.com/the-ai-hierarchy-of-needs-18f111fcc007**

Chapter 2 – 7 Principles of an AI Journey

1. Marr, Bernard. Forbes. 14 June 2019. *The Amazing Ways Hitachi Uses Artificial Intelligence And Machine Learning.* **https://www. forbes.com/sites/bernardmarr/2019/06/14/the-amazing-ways-hitachi-uses-artificial-intelligence-and-machine-learning/#73f23ab53705**

2. Polachowska, Kaja. Neoteric. 6 June 2019. *12 Challenges of AI Adoption.* **Source: https://neoteric.eu/blog/12-challenges-of-ai-adoption/**

Chapter 3 – Getting Ready to Use AI

1. Bayern, Macy. Tech Republic. 24 May 2019. *96% of organizations run into problems with AI and machine learning projects.* **Source: https://www.techrepublic.com/article/96-of-organizations-run-into-problems-with-ai-and-machine-learning-projects/**

2. Singh, Tarry. Forbes. 22 October 2018. *Artificial Intelligence In Enterprises - Businesses Are Waking Up.* **Source: https://www.forbes.com/sites/cognitiveworld/2018/10/22/artificial-intelligence-in-enterprises-businesses-are-waking-up/#693e06d13cb2**

3. Kantor, Bob. CIO. 30 January 2018. *The RACI Matrix: Your Blueprint for Project Success.* **Source: https://www.cio.com/article/2395825/project-management-how-to-design-a-successful-raci-project-plan.html**

4. *Microsoft. Causality and Machine Learning.* **Source: https://www.microsoft.com/en-us/research/group/causal-inference/**

5. Knight, Will. Wired. 10 August 2019. *An AI Pioneer Wants His Algorithms to Understand the 'Why'.* **Source: https://www.wired.com/story/ai-pioneer-algorithms-understand-why/**

Chapter 4 – Inside the AI Laboratory

1. Balatsko, Maksym. Towards Data Science. 29 May 2019. *All you want to know about preprocessing: Data preparation.* **Source: https://towardsdatascience.com/all-you-want-to-know-about-preprocessing-data-preparation-b6c2866071d4**

2. Peng, Tony & Sarazen, Michael. Medium. 5 December 2018. *Chinese Publisher Introduces AI Textbooks For Preschoolers.* **Source: https://medium.com/syncedreview/chinese-publisher-introduces-ai-textbooks-for-preschoolers-b95e1a89cfa0**

3. Vincent, James. The Verge. 5 March 2019. *Forty percent of 'AI startups' in Europe don't actually use AI, claims report.* **Source: https://www.theverge.com/2019/3/5/18251326/ai-startups-europe-fake-40-percent-mmc-report**

Chapter 5 – How AI Predicts Values and Categories

1. Hallman, Jessica. Science Daily. 2 July 2019. *Using artificial intelligence to better predict severe weather.* **Source: https://www. sciencedaily.com/releases/2019/07/190702160115.html**

2. Wiggers, Kyle. VentureBeat. 29 October 2019. *Facebook highlights AI that converts 2D objects into 3D shapes.* **Source: https://venturebeat.com/2019/10/29/facebook-highlights-ai-that-converts-2d-objects-into-3d-shapes/**

3. Perez, Sarah. Tech Crunch. 25 April 2019. *Walmart unveils an AI-powered store of the future, now open to the public.* **Source: https://techcrunch.com/2019/04/25/walmart-unveils-an-a-i-powered-store-of-the-future-now-open-to-the-public/**

4. Shotton, Jamie; Fitzgibbon, Andrew; Cook, Mat; Sharp, Toby; Finocchio, Mark; Moore, Richard; Kipman, Alex; Blake, Andrew. Microsoft. *Real-Time Human Pose Recognition in Parts from Single Depth Images.* **Source: https://www. microsoft.com/en-us/research/wp-content/uploads/2016/02/ BodyPartRecognition.pdf**

5. Buckley, Jay, and Dudley, Thomas J. Graziadio Business Review. *How Gerber Used a Decision Tree in Strategic Decision-Making.* **Source: https://gbr.pepperdine.edu/2010/08/how-gerber-used-a-decision-tree-in-strategic-decision-making/**

Chapter 6 – How AI Learns and Predicts Behaviors and Scenarios

1. Raghupathi, Kaushik. DZone. 27 March 2018. *10 Interesting Use Cases for the K-Means Algorithm.* **Source: https://dzone. com/articles/10-interesting-use-cases-for-the-k-means-algorithm**

2. Morgan, Blake. Forbes. 25 April 2019. *20 Examples Of Machine Learning Used In Customer Experience.* **Source: https://www.forbes.com/sites/blakemorgan/2019/04/25/20-examples-of-machine-learning-used-in-customer-experience/#5d9004db4052**

3. Bodern, Jim. Borden's Blather. 7 December 2018. *Beer and Diapers – the Perfect Couple.* **Source: https://jborden. com/2018/12/07/beer-and-diapers-the-perfect-couple/**

4. Roell, Jason. Medium. 29 September 2017. *Why AlphaGo is a bigger game-changer for Artificial Intelligence than many realize.*

Source: https://medium.com/@roelljr/why-alpha-go-is-a-bigger-game-changer-for-artificial-intelligence-than-many-realize-64b00f54a0

Chapter 7 – How AI Communicates and Learns from Mistakes

1. Cuttler, Marcy. CBC. 26 April 2019. *Transforming health care: How artificial intelligence is reshaping the medical landscape.* Source: https://www.cbc.ca/news/health/artificial-intelligence-health-care-1.5110892

2. Hao, Karen. MIT Technology Review. 15 January 2020. *An algorithm that learns through rewards may show how our brain does too.* **Source:** https://www.technologyreview.com/s/615054/deepmind-ai-reiforcement-learning-reveals-dopamine-neurons-in-brain/

3. Hao, Karen. MIT Technology Review. 15 January 2020. *An algorithm that learns through rewards may show how our brain does too.* **Source:** https://www.technologyreview.com/s/615054/deepmind-ai-reiforcement-learning-reveals-dopamine-neurons-in-brain/

4. Nosta, John. Fortune. 7 May 2019. *A.I. Can Now Read Your Thoughts—And Turn Them Into Words and Images.* **Source:** https://fortune.com/2019/05/07/artificial-intelligence-mind-reading-technology/

5. Kucera, Roman. Towards Data Science. 7 August 2017. *The truth behind Facebook AI inventing a new language.* **Source:** https://towardsdatascience.com/the-truth-behind-facebook-ai-inventing-a-new-language-37c5d680e5a7

Chapter 8 – How AI Starts to Think Like Humans

1. Cox, Laura. Disruption Hub. 5 April 2017. 5 *Amazing Things IBM's Watson Can Do.* **Source:** https://disruptionhub.com/5-amazing-things-ibms-watson-can/

2. Somers, James. The New Yorker. 28 December 2018. *How the Artificial Intelligence Program AlphaZero Mastered Its Games.* **Source:** https://www.newyorker.com/science/elements/how-the-artificial-intelligence-program-alphazero-mastered-its-games

3. Desjardin, Jeff. VisualCapitalist. 15 April 2019. *How Much Data is Generated Each Day?* **Source: https://www.visualcapitalist. com/how-much-data-is-generated-each-day/**

4. Loechner, Jack. Research Brief. 22 December 2016. *90% Of Today's Data Created In Two Years.* **Source: https://www. mediapost.com/publications/article/291358/90-of-todays-data-created-in-two-years.html**

5. Shankland, Stephen. CNet. 29 June 2019. *Startup packs all 16GB of Wikipedia onto DNA strands to demonstrate new storage tech.* **Source: https://www.cnet.com/news/startup-packs-all-16gb-wikipedia-onto-dna-strands-demonstrate-new-storage-tech/**

6. Extance, Andy. Nature. 2 September 2016. *How DNA could store all the world's data.* **Source: https://www.nature.com/ news/how-dna-could-store-all-the-world-s-data-1.20496**

7. Hartnet, Kevin. Quanta Magazine. 18 July 2019. *Quantum Supremacy Is Coming: Here's What You Should Know.* **Source: https://www.quantamagazine.org/quantum-supremacy-is-coming-heres-what-you-should-know-20190718/**

8. Ross, Valerie. Discover. 14 May 2011. *Numbers: The Nervous System, From 268-MPH Signals to Trillions of Synapses.* **Source: https://www.discovermagazine.com/health/numbers-the-nervous-system-from-268-mph-signals-to-trillions-of-synapses**

9. Dickson, Ben. VentureBeat. 28 July 2019. *Deep learning is about to get easier and more widespread.* **Source: https://venturebeat. com/2019/07/28/deep-learning-is-about-to-get-easier-and-more-widespread/**

10. Greenwald, John. Princeton University. 17 April 2019. *Artificial intelligence accelerates efforts to develop clean, virtually limitless fusion energy.* **Source: https://www.princeton.edu/ news/2019/04/17/artificial-intelligence-accelerates-efforts-develop-clean-virtually-limitless**

11. Fisher, Christine. Endgadget. 24 October 2019. *Google researchers taught an AI to recognize smells.* **Source: https:// www.engadget.com/2019/10/24/google-researchers-train-ai-smells/**

12. Kurzweil, Ray. *Futurism. The Dawn of the Singularity.* **Source: https://futurism.com/images/the-dawn-of-the-singularity**

13. Feldman, Michael. The Next Platform. 26 July 2019. *The Singularity is nearer: Microsoft places $1 billion bet on Artificial General Intelligence.* **Source: https://www.nextplatform. com/2019/07/26/the-singularity-is-nearer-microsoft-places-1-billion-bet-on-artificial-general-intelligence/**

14. Wang, Yuxuan. Google AI Blog. 27 March 2018. *Expressive Speech Synthesis with Tacotron.* **Source: https://ai.googleblog. com/2018/03/expressive-speech-synthesis-with.html**

15. Kalash, Mahmoud; Rochan, Mrigank; Mohammed, Noman; D. B. Bruce, Neil; Wang, Yang; and Iqbal, Farkhund. IEEE. 2 April 2018. *Malware Classification with Deep Convolutional Neural Networks.* **Source: https://ieeexplore.ieee.org/ document/8328749**

Chapter 9 – AI Adoption and Valuation

1. Casado, Martin, and Bornstein, Matt. Andreessen Horowitz. 16 February 2020. *The New Business of AI (and How It's Different From Traditional Software).* **Source: https://a16z. com/2020/02/16/the-new-business-of-ai-and-how-its-different-from-traditional-software/**

2. Kerr, Evan. Georgian Partners. 30 January 2020. *The Metrics that Matter for Growth Stage Startups in 2020.* **Source: https:// growth.georgianpartners.com/c/the-metrics-that-mat**

3. Bates, Alex. The Next Web. 15 July 2019. *Nations must double down on AI R&D — or risk falling behind.* **Source: https:// thenextweb.com/podium/2019/07/15/nations-must-double-down-on-ai-rd-or-risk-falling-behind/**

4. Columbus, Louis. Forbes. 25 September 2019. *What's New In Gartner's Hype Cycle For AI, 2019.* **Source: https://www. forbes.com/sites/louiscolumbus/2019/09/25/whats-new-in-gartners-hype-cycle-for-ai-2019/#3e261f96547b**

5. Ratnam, Gopal. The Star. 15 June 2019. *Artificial intelligence is coming: Will politicians be ready?* **Source: https://www.thestar. com.my/tech/tech-news/2019/06/16/artificial-intelligence-is-coming-will-politicians-be-ready/**

Chapter 10 – AI Strategy, Policy and Risk Management

1. Google. *Responsible AI Practices*. **Source: https://ai.google/ responsibilities/responsible-ai-practices/**

2. Kanso, Heba. Global News. 4 November 2017. *Saudi Arabia gave 'citizenship' to a robot named Sophia, and Saudi women aren't amused*. **Source: https://globalnews.ca/news/3844031/ saudi-arabia-robot-citizen-sophia/**

3. Ferreira, Victor. Financial Post. 3 June 2019. *Artificial intelligence can now pick stocks and build portfolios. Are human managers about to be replaced?* **Source: https://business.financialpost. com/investing/artificial-intelligence-can-now-pick-stocks- and-build-portfolios-are-human-managers-about-to-be- replaced**

4. CBC Cross Country Checkup. CBC. 3 September 2017. *When milking robots were installed, this dairy farm worker's fears vanished quickly.* **Source: http://www.cbc.ca/radio/checkup/ blog/when-milking-robots-were-installed-this-dairy-farm- worker-s-fears-vanished-quickly-1.4274643**

5. Reed, Elodie. The Atlantic. 11 October 2018. *The Cow-Milking Robots Keeping Small Farms in Business.* **Source: https://www. theatlantic.com/business/archive/2018/10/young-dairy- farmers/567937/**

6. Brean, Joseph. The National Post. 6 June 2019. *How do you teach a machine right from wrong? Addressing the morality within Artificial Intelligence.* **Source: https://nationalpost.com/ feature/how-do-you-teach-a-machine-right-from-wrong- addressing-the-morality-within-artificial-intelligence**

7. Ratnam, Gopal. The Star. 15 June 2019. *Artificial intelligence is coming: Will politicians be ready?* **Source: https://www.thestar. com.my/tech/tech-news/2019/06/16/artificial-intelligence- is-coming-will-politicians-be-ready/**

8. Solsman, Joan E. CNet. 24 May 2019. *Samsung deepfake AI could fabricate a video of you from a single profile pic.* **Source: https:// www.cnet.com/news/samsung-ai-deepfake-can-fabricate- a-video-of-you-from-a-single-photo-mona-lisa-cheapfake- dumbfake/**

9. Coldewey, David. TechCrunch. 10 June 2019. *To detect fake news, this AI first learned to write it.* **Source: https://techcrunch.**

com/2019/06/10/to-detect-fake-news-this-ai-first-learned-to-write-it/

10. Cuttler, Marcy. CBC. 26 April 2019. *Transforming health care: How artificial intelligence is reshaping the medical landscape.* **Source:** **https://www.cbc.ca/news/health/artificial-intelligence-health-care-1.5110892**

11. Vincent, James. The Verge. 27 January 2020. *Why Cancer-spotting AI needs to be handled with care.* **Source: https://www.theverge.com/2020/1/27/21080253/ai-cancer-diagnosis-dangers-mammography-google-paper-accuracy**

Made in United States
North Haven, CT
03 July 2024

54381091R00104